It is my sincere desire that the owner of this book would find within the pages healing that only comes from our loving and caring Abba-daddy!

I speak a blessing over your life that you will come to know your Abba-daddy in the full measure of his abiding mercy and power that is available to his children.

Sincerely in His Service,

Your Sister and Your Father's Daughter

Notice is hereby given that this author claims the full trade-mark rights to the all inferences of the "Salvation "Soteria" More Than a Ticket to Heaven", the "Ticket to Heaven" utilized throughout the various books, tapes and any and all electronic media used to convey the Salvation "Soteria" More Than A Ticket to Heaven Message.

© 2012, Patricia E. Adams

Copyright © 2012 by Patricia E. Adams

Printed and bound in the United States of America. All rights reserved. No part of this book may be reproduced or transmitted in any form or by any means, electronic or mechanical, including photocopying, recording, or by an information storage and retrieval system -- except by a reviewer who may quote brief passages in a review to be printed in a magazine or newspaper -- without permission in writing from the publisher. For information please contact Shekinah Publishing House, 877/538-1363. Although the author and publisher have made every effort to ensure the accuracy and completeness of information contained in this book, we assume no responsibility for errors, inaccuracies, omissions, or any inconsistency herein. Any slights of people, places, or organizations are unintentional.

Scripture quotations are from the KING JAMES
VERSION of the Bible.
Printed in the United States of America
ISBN 09700976-4-6
LCCN 99090791
Salvation "Soteria - Unpack It and Use It: It's More Than a Ticket To Heaven

---

ATTENTION ORGANIZATIONS, HEALING CENTERS, AND SCHOOLS OF SPIRITUAL DEVELOPMENT:
Quantity discounts are available on bulk purchases of this book for educational purposes. Special books or book excerpts can also be created to fit specific needs. For information, please contact Shekinah Publishing House, 1-877/538-1363.

Patricia E. Adams is a Christian, Speaker, Author, Mentor, Instructor, Coach, Leader, Children's Rights Advocate, Domestic Violence Advocate and Internet Radio Host.

She serves in her local church and community and a portion of her titles are series, one of which is called "The One Heart Series,' "The Set Free to Praise Him Series" and two upcoming series in development at this writing. She writes about the salvation journey as a process of becoming intimate with God.

There are five (5) books currently in the One Heart Series; and 1 (one) in the Set Free to Praise Him Series with four (4) additional titles. God has placed a strong gift of teaching within her that speaks the truth in love, with a commandment to draw his people out and into an intimate relationship with their God.

God has wrought a mighty deliverance in her life from the baggage of physical, sexual, emotional, and religious bondage. Her testimony is that God is a mighty Deliverer and Restorer. Patricia is available to share her testimony of deliverance and restoration to groups across the country and around the world.

Lectures/Seminars/Workshops/Keynotes
Writing & Publishing Seminars
Intellectual Property Workshops
Family Seminars (Men, Women and Children)
Ministry of Helps

Please contact her for additional information at

Email: author@oneheartseries.com Radio Network: www.blogtalkradio.com/patricia-adams-live

Website: www.oneheartseries.com

This book is dedicated to the Ministers of the Gospel -

Reflection of My Salvation Journey

My first recall of asking Jesus into my life was during Sunday School Class and we were studying from the picture card that showed Jesus on the front knocking on a door! We, the children in the class were probably 4 or 5 years old at the time. When the teacher asked if we wanted to be saved after she finished explaining the card most of us raised our hands and accepted this gift of salvation! Did I understand completely what happened that day? No! Shortly thereafter I recall being baptized in this huge baptismal pool by the Pastor and people were seated looking on! Shortly after that my mother was murdered and I did not give God or the gift of salvation any forethought! It was four years later that I recall accepting this same free gift of salvation at the age of 9 in the bathroom of the new family I was living with. But this time there was a better understanding of what I was saying. By this time I had been exposed to a different denominations viewpoint and obviously being older affected my experience this time. Also, I had prayed a prayer to Jesus asking him not to let something happen and he to me answered the prayer! After seeing this answer I asked him into my life and he came in and filled me with the Holy Spirit and the evidence of speaking in tongues! From 9 until 16 I maintained my faith in the midst of great chaos! From the age of 17 to 18, I began to question my experience because too much chaos had been inflicted on my life that was unfair. From 18 through 25 I wavered and backslid and turned away from the Church, but somehow longed to understand the God of my salvation. By his grace he kept me during this wavering and I came back for 5 years, but turned away again when the local church leader fell! At the age of 31, God seemed to have had enough of my backslidings and confronted me with his PRESENCE in a tangible way! From that day until now I have loved Him and known Him so deeply that my mind is made up and my heart is fixed – no turning back – no turning back! It is with this fervor that this book is born to give an account of salvation that will cause you to keep your eyes fixed on him and not the people around you! Be free in the matchless and marvelous name of the lover of your soul Jesus Christ!" Again, may you find restoration and wholeness on every page for your life!

Table of Contents

Reflection of My Salvation Journey xi
1- Order out of Chaos 3
2- Now Are We Sons 41
3- Obey and It Will Go Well 53
4- Give Me Something to Pour Into 81
5- The Plan of Salvation 97
6- The Process of Salvation 113
Salvations Ladder 121
Biblical Numbers Significance 123
Step 1 Propitiation 124
Step 2 - Redemption 127
Step 3 - Reconciliation 129
Step 4 - Election 130
Step 5 - Calling 133
Step 6 - Regeneration 134
Step 7 - Conversion 140
Step 8 - Justification 141
Step 9 - Adoption 144
Step 10 - Union with Christ 145
Step 11 - Sanctification 156
Step 12 - Perseverance 166
Step 13 - Glorification 176
Step 14 – Salvation 179
7- The Mount of Transfiguration 183
Changing the Guard 190

8- Original Sin	199
Components of Salvation One(ness)	210
Reconciliation	215
Our Lives after the Cross	216
9- A Justified Man -	223
(Obedience)	227
Enlarging Your Tent Prayer -	231
Cleansed and Salted - Ezekiel 16:4	233
The Robe of Many Colors	234
Glory to Glory – Level of the Relationship	236
The Inner Court Relationship	239
Brazen Altar	240
The Holy Place	241
The Unlimited Presence	242
The Veil of the Tabernacle	244
Ark of the Covenant	244
The Ten Commandments	244
For All Times	246
10- Where There is Bitterness	253
What Is In the Name of Jesus' Lineage	261
The Fear of the Lord	271
Reverence of God	273
Authority and Fatherhood	275
Sonship and Obedience	276
The Fragrance of the Relationship	282
Flies in the Ointments Ecclesiastes 10:1	285
Pre-Extrication	286
A Time of Death and Bondage	287

Sins of Lust 287

Sins of Divination and False Worship 288

Sins of Anger 288

Sins of the Stomach 289

The Prodigal Son and the Older Brother 290

Post-extrication 291

In the Care of God 295

The Zoe 297

Endnotes 301

Volumes in the One Heart Series 303

Other Books by Patricia E. Adams 305

Chapter 1
Order out of Chaos

1- Order out of Chaos

Order, Order, Order in the Court – the Judge demands with the pounding of his gavel! And if order does not ensue the court personnel will enforce the Judges demands by any means necessary!

This is earthly order, but what about divine order? We borrow from the One Heart Series an Inductive Study on Intimacy with God a timeless truth!

What is divine order? It is the ability to remain in the center of Gods' will, dwelling, stable and fixed no matter what the circumstances! Some of us accomplish this and others falter and others pursue feverishly to get to the center of God's will!

The indwelling and infilling of the Holy Spirit is the psuche of God that leads and guides us into all truth, according to John Chapter 16. Jesus is telling his disciples that he will be leaving them soon because he has accomplished that which his Father sent him to accomplish. It is through this message that the servants begin to feel sorrowful for themselves and had not yet discerned the hour or the full purpose of Jesus Christ and His Anointing!

For the scripture records the discourse as follows in John 16:7-33 (KJV):

Nevertheless I tell you the truth; It is expedient for you that I go away: for if I go not away, the Comforter will not come unto you; but if I depart, I will send him unto you. 8 And when he is come, he will reprove the world of sin, and of righteousness, and of judgment: 9 Of sin, because they believe not on me; 10 Of righteousness, because I go to my Father, and ye see me no more; **11** *Of judgment, because the prince of this world is judged.* **12** *I have yet many things to say unto you, but ye cannot bear them now.* **13** *Howbeit when he, the Spirit of truth, is come, he will guide you into all truth: for he shall not speak of himself; but whatsoever he shall hear, that shall he speak: and he will shew you things to come.* **14** *He shall glorify me: for he shall receive of mine, and shall shew it unto you.* **15** *All things that the Father hath are mine: therefore said I, that he shall take of mine, and shall shew it unto you.* **16** *A little while, and ye shall not see me: and again, a little while, and ye shall see me, because I go to the Father.* **17** *Then said some of his disciples among themselves, What is this that he saith unto us, A little while, and ye shall not see me: and again, a little while, and ye shall see me: and, Because I go to the Father?* **18** *They said therefore, What is this that he saith, A little while? we cannot tell what he saith.* **19** *Now Jesus knew that they were desirous* to ask him, and said unto them, *Do ye enquire among yourselves of that I said, A little while, and ye shall not see me: and again, a little while, and ye shall see me?* **20** *Verily, verily, I say unto you, That ye shall weep and lament, but the world shall rejoice: and ye shall be sorrowful, but your sorrow shall be turned into joy.* **21** *A woman when she is in travail hath sorrow, because her hour is come: but as soon as she is delivered of the child, she remembereth no more the anguish, for joy that a man is born into the world.* **22** *And ye now therefore have sorrow: but I will see you again, and your heart shall rejoice, and your joy no man taketh from you.*

He assures them that their prayers made in His name will be answered by His Father

23 And in that day ye shall ask me nothing. Verily, verily, I say unto you, Whatsoever ye shall ask the Father in my name, he will give it you. 24 Hitherto have ye asked nothing in my

name: ask, and ye shall receive, that your joy may be full. 25 These things have I spoken unto you in proverbs: but the time cometh, when I shall no more speak unto you in proverbs, but I shall shew you plainly of the Father. 26 At that day ye shall ask in my name: and I say not unto you, that I will pray the Father for you: 27 For the Father himself loveth you, because ye have loved me, and have believed that I came out from God. 28 I came forth from the Father, and am come into the world: again, I leave the world, and go to the Father. 29 His disciples said unto him, Lo, now speakest thou plainly, and speakest no proverb. 30 Now are we sure that thou knowest all things, and needest not that any man should ask thee: by this we believe that thou camest forth from God. 31 Jesus answered them, Do ye now believe? 32 Behold, the hour cometh, yea, is now come, that ye shall be scattered, every man to his own, and shall leave me alone: and yet I am not alone, because the Father is with me. 33 These things I have spoken unto you, that in me ye might have peace. In the world ye shall have tribulation: but be of good cheer; I have overcome the world.

Jesus has poured himself and is continously pouring himself out and shall not cease; unless he chooses to stop the outpouring on all flesh. Through this we are empowered to take auhority and bring order into the chaos of our lives. By asking the Father in Jesus's Name according to the power that works in us and wills to do through the Word of God!

We have been endowed or endued with the life producing breath of God to keep all that has been given us from the original beginning of man!

In Genesis 1:26-28 God said to himselves by opening the passage with 'said' once, and then God 'created' three times and God 'blessed' once and God closes with 'said' unto those he made in his image what their responsibilities towards everything else he had created not in his image.

Order was spoken into Chaos, it was implemented through the authority of the word of God's mouth as follows:

Genesis 1:26 And God said, Let us make man in our image, after our likeness: and let them have dominion over the fish of the sea, and over the fowl of the air, and over the cattle, and over all the earth, and over every creeping thing that creepeth upon the earth. 27 So God created man in his own image, in the image of God created he him; male and female created he them. 28 And God blessed them, and God said unto them, Be fruitful, and multiply, and replenish the earth, and subdue it: and have dominion over the fish of the sea, and over the fowl of the air, and over every living thing that moveth upon the earth.

If we go to Hebrews 1:1-3 we find the confirmation of this Old Testament passage:

1 God, who at sundry times and in divers manners spake in time past unto the fathers by the prophets, 2 Hath in these last days spoken unto us by his Son, whom he hath appointed heir of all things, by whom also he made the worlds; 3 Who being the brightness of his glory, and the express image of his person, and upholding all things by the word of his power, when he had by himself purged our sins, sat down on the right hand of the Majesty on high;" and It is through the power of his word that he upholds all things to this very day and keeps the house of the universe in order. Even thought there are wars and rumors of wars and all types of evil present!

If God were not maintaining the order given to us through the death, burial, resurrection and ascencion of his son Jesus Christ our worlds would collide and we would no longer exist!

The Word of God says in II Thessalonians 2:7, "For the mystery of iniquity doth already work: only he who now letteth will let, until he be taken out of the way." And in Heb 10:37-39 37 For yet a little while, and he that shall come will come, and will not tarry. 38 Now the just shall live by faith: but if any man draw back, my soul shall have no pleasure in him. 39 But we are not of them who draw back unto perdition; but of them that believe to the saving of the soul."

Until that day we will have tribulations but his return will be when He decides!

Meanwhile, we become enabled to live the God-life, that is the Zoe life through the gift of salvation.

Romans Chapter 10, Paul expresses his desire of God for them is that they would all be saved:

"Brethren, my heart's desire and prayer to God for Israel is, that they might be saved. 2 For I bear them record that they have a zeal of God, but not according to knowledge. 3 For they being ignorant of God's righteousness, and going about to establish their own righteousness, have not submitted themselves unto the righteousness of God. 4 For Christ is the end of the law for righteousness to every one that believeth. 5 For Moses describeth the righteousness which is of the law, That the man which doeth those things shall live by them. 6 But the righteousness which is of faith speaketh on this wise, Say not in thine heart, Who shall ascend into heaven? (that is, to bring Christ down from above:) 7 Or, Who shall descend into the deep? (that is, to bring up Christ again from the dead.) 8 But what saith it? The word is nigh thee, even in thy mouth, and in thy heart: that is, the word of faith, which we preach; 9 That if thou shalt confess with thy mouth the Lord Jesus, and shalt believe in thine heart that God hath raised him from the dead, thou shalt be saved. 10 For with the heart man believeth unto righteousness; and with the mouth confession is made unto salvation. 11 For the scripture saith, Whosoever believeth on him shall not be ashamed. 12 For there is no difference between the Jew and the Greek: for the same Lord over all is rich unto all that call upon him. 13 For whosoever shall call upon the name of the Lord shall be saved. 14 How then shall they call on him in whom they have not believed? and how shall they believe in him of whom they have not heard? and how shall they hear without a preacher? 15 And how shall they preach, except they be sent? as it is written, How beautiful are the feet of them that preach the gospel of peace, and bring glad tidings of good things! 16 But they have not all obeyed the gospel. For Esaias saith, Lord, who hath believed our report? 17 So then faith cometh by hearing, and hearing by the word of God. 18 But I say, Have they not heard? Yes verily, their sound went into all the earth, and their words unto the ends of the world. 19 But I say, Did not Israel know? First Moses saith, I will provoke you to jealousy by them that are no people, and by a foolish nation I will anger you. 20 But Esaias is very bold, and saith, I was found of them that sought me not; I was made manifest unto them that asked not after me. 21 But to Israel he saith, All day long I have stretched forth my hands unto a disobedient and gainsaying people."

The free gift was sought after by those who were 'no people' and a 'foolish nation' in spite of the plan of salvation being for the nation of Israel. Through their disobedience and the gentiles called upon the name of their Lord and were engrafted into the true vine! We are now children by adoption, and sons by one way that was made through one mans obedience unto the death!

The way of salvation is the path of obedience, through obedience we become the sons of God!

We are his children through the free gift of salvation and his sons through our obedience to the gospel. Not all obeyed!

Yet we who choose to obey are in possession in our spirit man of the desire to aim intentionally after the prize of a high calling recorded in Phillipians 3:13-14, " Brethren, I count not myself to have apprehended: but this one thing I do, forgetting those things which are behind, and reaching forth unto those things which are before, 14 I press toward the mark for the prize of the high calling of God in Christ Jesus."

Pursuing peace and follow after holiness is the way we put on the gift of salvation according to Hebrews 10:12-16 ""Wherefore lift up the hands which hang down, and the feeble knees; 13 And make straight paths for your feet, lest that which is lame be turned out of the way; but let it rather be healed. 14 Follow peace with all men, and holiness, without which no man shall see the

Lord: 15 Looking diligently lest any man fail of the grace of God; lest any root of bitterness springing up trouble you, and thereby many be defiled; 16 Lest there be any fornicator, or profane person, as Esau, who for one morsel of meat sold his birthright."

No longer gainsayers but holding the sole aim and desire to pursue perfectly and sincerely after the heart of God according to Genesis 2:7.

What areas of your life are out of order and chaotic? Throughout time, it has required the repetitive action of conception to reproduce man in the earth, being birthed from deep within woman.

However, God has gone above repetitive natural conception, and required spiritual conception and birth through his death, burial and resurrection of Jesus. Through whom we gain and maintain access to our divine inheritance and God! Through his death, the seed of salvation is planted. Through the burial, the soil of the heart is broken open by the birth of the seed of salvation, and the heart of God is received.

Through the resurrection that transplanted seed and beating heart is pushed through into the earth as a new creation, and thus multiplying after it's kind. Becoming a member of the family of God and the household of faith!

Reminds you of the birth of a baby, doesn't it! Unless you wanted to become stale and stunted in your development; once you are born again, you have to feed on the milk of the Word of God. And then one day you become able to stand before the world, with the heart of God being expressed toward the nations. Remember the Bible says there will come a time when you will need to teach and not always be a student! It is now required of man to be born again from deep within the life of God to gain and maintain access to our divine inheritance. You are now operating in the providence of God; the preservation, provision and governance of God that pertains to life and godliness.

The heart of God must be received and transplanted within us. We are not able to stand perfect and upright without his heart, a perfect heart.

The heart of God in Acts 11:23, in the natural realm enables us to bridge the imperfections of our flesh and enter into the place and posture of holiness.

For the Word of God says that in Him we live, move, and have our being.

He replaces our weaknesses with his strength, and thereby become perfect in purpose. Enabled and equipped for the work of God.

God gave Eve the right of way into Adam's heart. A connection from God had been engrafted into her through Adams' rib. Eve touched Adam and affected him in a way that the rest of his creation could not. Have you noticed how some women can tear men down, and others can build them up! Well that's why!

A woman's words were meant to reach into a man's heart and prophesy the heart of his vision. Creating an environment that is conducive for impregnation and production from the seed of faith. Thus if she is tearing her man down; she is operating in the flesh and psychic power. Because psychic power is Satan's version of the prophetic gift from God.

The Bible tells us that it is better for a man to dwell in the corner of the top of the house than in the house, with a contentious woman. Because she will frustrate his purpose and thwart his dreams and visions. Society has created categories, classes and degrees of natural and physical beauty. Their beauty is temporal and based on feelings that are temporal.

God can take what is ugly in societies eyes and beautify them without the use of artificial substances. He is after all the first plastic surgeon, he works from the inside out, and his work is for eternity! We look at the things which are seen and become stimulated to the point of obsession over an outwardly attractive person, and once we take the wrapper off and play with it a little while; the beast appears and then it is too late to withdraw! There are beautiful people who are beautiful through and through and there is nothing wrong with that!

But when your number one criteria is to seek after the flesh of that person and not their spirit, you are asking for a double dose of misery.

Satan perverts and blinds us with the secret desires of our hearts to keep us from walking in the divine order of God for our lives. An old adage I heard as a child; goes something like this "Beauty is only skin deep, but ugly is to the bone." As a child, I did not understand this, but as I have lived life a little longer, I have my own interpretation.

Just because the package looks good on the outside, does not mean that it is; and ugliness is found in the core "the bone" of a human being's character, and it is hard to miss. When a woman's husband leaves for another woman less attractive than she is. She becomes highly offended, but more than anything it creates a large void deep within her that makes her question her own beauty; and thus she becomes subconsciously insecure.

She wonders and exclaims to anyone who will listen, 'what does he see in her?'

What she has failed to realize the less attractive woman may have spent more time on her inner beauty, and thus displays a certain confidence outwardly to others than her "more attractive" counterpart. What is on the inside of a person will show up on the outside, sooner or later.

I heard another saying as a child that said a less attractive woman tries harder, and is generally of a sweeter disposition.

Now what I am trying to convey to you is this; don't be distracted from God's purpose for your life by an outward, temporary housing that is subject to change with time. So ladies and gents if you have been conducting your own taste test by feasting on a platter full of ribs; instead of the one rib God ordained for you; then how can you expect for your life to be anything else but shambles.

Note in Genesis 2:23, and 20 that the woman was known as Adam before the fall; meaning they were one and the same, with one heart rhythm, they were synchronized if you will.

Woman was born in the image of God, from "within" man, from his inner man, which symbolizes the soul and heart. Hence, woman is an innermost vessel (Genesis 2:18-22).

Let's reiterate this passage from chapter one, that as a sign and result of their ONENESS, man perpetually is born of a woman.

This is why Adam named her "Eve" the mother of all living. She is the receiver and carrier internally, physically and spiritually of their unity (Genesis 4:1-2).

This is why we as Temples of the Holy Ghost are carriers of our unity with God!

Oneness is being in possession of the intent, and aim to do what Jesus says, what Jesus speaks, what Jesus hears as the Holy Spirit translates it to us in our earthly language.

II King 20:35, says that Hezekiah turned his face to the wall and prayed, saying "...O Lord, remember now how I have walked before thee in truth and with a perfect heart, and have done that which is good in thy sight. Isaiah...turn again and tell Hezekiah...I have heard thy prayer...seen thy tears...I will heal thee."

David a man after God's own heart told his son Solomon, the wisest man alive in I Chronicles 28:9 to be sure and serve him with a perfect heart and a willing mind. For he (David) knew that the Lord searched all hearts, and understood all the imaginations of the thoughts; if thou seek him, he will be found of thee; but if thou forsake him, he will cast thee off for ever. (Ecclesiastes 12:13)

David said in Psalms 37:31 that this man, who has the law of his God in his heart; will see none of his steps slide. Jeremiah said in Chapter 32:39, "...that those who do these things will be his people, and he their God, and I will give them one heart, and one way, that they may fear me forever, for the good of them, and of their children after them...I will put my fear in their hearts, that they shall not depart from me...yea, I will rejoice over them to do them good, and I will plant them in this land assuredly with my whole heart and with my whole soul." God loves us with his whole heart, and to effectively communicate and access the kingdom of God we must likewise, as his creations love him.

The most fulfilling time in a Christians life is in, Acts 11:23 "...that with purpose of heart they would 'cleave' to the Lord." Order in its' pure form can not exist without God in our lives! We have a form of godliness that denies the power thereof. The word in Hebrew 'Dabaq' means to cleave, to be attached, devoted, and to hang upon.

One who dabaqs' God can be built upon as a church that the gates of hell can not prevail against!

Before God could create in the earth, he brought order and dispersed the chaos! The Hebrew word for this type of order can be seen in the word cleave, but this is not dabaq but Baqa – to divide, lay open, hatch, break in upon. Genesis 1:2 says "And the earth was without form, and void; and darkness was upon the face of the deep.

Moreover, the spirit of God moved upon the face of the waters. And God said, Let there be light: and there was light."

Without the spirit of God moving up on the face of the waters of your life there is total chaos! You must decide whose side you are on – not tomorrow, but right now! Because the further you go into this study the more you will know, and the more God will require of you. God has birthed this material out of me through obedience, and it has not all been without pain. Therefore, an anointing of obedience is upon you as you read this material, to cause you to do that which you should do, not what you use to do. I hope you have chosen to stay on the Lord's side or get on the Lord's side. I John 2:4 "He that saith, I know him, and keepeth not his commandments, is a liar, and the truth is not in him."

Divine order in a believer's life is the whole duty of man according to Ecclesiastes 12:13 "Let us hear the conclusion of the whole matter: Fear God, and keep his commandments: for this is the whole duty of man"

A life of divine order will bring ..."The Commanded Blessing," found in Deuteronomy

28:1:14:"AND IT shall come to pass, if thou hearken diligently unto the voice of the Lord thy God, to observe and to do all his commandments which I command thee this day,...that the Lord thy God will set thee on high above all nations of the earth: And all these blessings shall come on thee, and overtake thee, if thou shalt hearken unto the voice of the Lord thy God.

The Commanded Blessing says that,

- *Blessed shalt thou be in the city, and blessed shalt thou be in the field.*

- *Blessed shall be the fruit of thy body, and the fruit of thy ground, and the fruit of thy cattle, the increase of thy kine, and the flocks of thy sheep.*

- *Blessed shall be thy basket and thy store.*

- *Blessed shalt thou be when thou comest in, and blessed shalt thou be when thou goest out.*

The Lord shall cause thine enemies that rise up against thee to be smitten before thy face: they shall come out against thee one way, and flee before thee seven ways.

The Lord shall command the blessing upon thee in thy storehouses, and in all that thou settest thine hand unto; and he shall bless thee in the land which the Lord thy God giveth thee.

The Lord shall establish thee an holy people unto himself, as he hath sworn unto thee, if thou shalt keep the commandments of the Lord thy God, and walk in his ways.

All people of the earth shall see that thou art called by the name of the Lord; and they shall be afraid of thee.

And the Lord shall make thee plenteous in goods, in the fruit of thy body, and in the fruit of the cattle and in the fruit of thy ground, in the land which the Lord sware unto thy fathers to give thee.

The Lord shall open unto thee his good treasure, the heaven to give the rain unto thy land in his season, and to bless all the work of thine hand: and thou shalt lend unto many nations, and thou shalt not borrow.

And the Lord shall make thee the head, and not the tail; and thou shalt be above only, and thou shalt not be beneath: if that thou hearken unto the commandments of the Lord thy God, which I command thee this day, to observe and to do them:

And thou shalt not go aside from any of the words which I command thee this day, to the right hand, or to the left, to go after other gods to serve them."

The patterned life of one who accepts, receives, and applies the divine order for his life is the righteous man who follows these steps:

"BLESSED IS the man that walketh not in the counsel of the ungodly, nor standeth in the way of sinners, nor sitteth in the seat of the scornful.

But his delight is in the law of the Lord; and in his law doth he meditate day and night.

And he shall be like a tree planted by the rivers of water, that bringeth forth his fruit in his season; his leaf also shall not wither; and whatsoever he doeth shall prosper...

BUT ...

...the ungodly are not so: but are like the chaff which the wind driveth away.

Therefore the ungodly shall not stand in the judgment, nor sinners in the congregation of the righteous.

For the Lord knoweth the way of the righteous; but the way of the ungodly shall perish."

A blessed man is an obedient man. That man is like a tree planted by the rivers of water. That man is not a sinner (oops) but a righteous man. One who practices the way of God and walks therein. The whole conclusion of God's purpose for our lives!

Everything else is the outworking of the inworking of Deuteronomy 28 and Psalms 1.

Your calling and election are manifestations of your inward walk of righteousness, and the method by which God chooses to express your inward walk. Such as Apostle, Prophet, Teacher, Evangelist, or Pastor.

The ability to operate with ease in these comes from the fruits of the spirit, which is the outward flow of your love walk.

The love of God is shed abroad from breast to breast! The gifts of the spirit operate like a gauge on a car measuring the amount of gas in your car.

The effectiveness of your gifts are a direct relationship to the measure of anointing in your life. Do do not get deep, and start looking around the room, and saying oh that is why sister and brother so and so is ineffective in their call.

My people perish for a lack of knowledge.

The anointing is increased as we spend time in prayer, praise, worship and studying of the Word (anointing in print) of God. (II Timothy 2:15)

I know that you have read that God gave gifts unto man as he deemed. But an illustration of whether you could handle additional gifts is found in Matthew 25 in the comparison of the three(3) servants.

Matthew 25:14-30 "For the kingdom of heaven is as a man travelling into a far country, who called his own servants, and delivered unto them his goods…Let's diagram this passage!

Servant 1: And unto one he gave five talents,

Servant 2: to another two,

Servant 3: and to another one;

... to every man according to his several ability; and straightway took his journey...

Servant 2: Then he that had received two, he also gained another two.

Servant 3: But he that had received one went and digged in the earth, and hid his lord's money.

...After a long time the lord of those servants cometh, and reckoneth with them.

Servant 1: And so he that received five talents came and brought other five...

His lord said unto him, well done,

thou good and faithful servant; thou hast been faithful over a few things,

...I will make you ruler over many things; enter thou into the joy of the lord.

Servant 2: He also that had received two talents came...behold I have gained two other talents.

... Well done thy good and faithful servant; thou hast been faithful over a few things,

 I will make thee ruler over many things: enter thou into the joy of thy Lord.

Servant 3: Then he which had received the one talent came and said...I was afraid, and hid thy talent...lo, there thou hast that is thine.

...His lord answered and said unto him, Thou wicked and slothful servant...take therefore the talent from him, and give it unto him which hath ten talents...And cast ye the unprofitable servant into outer darkness: there shall be weeping and gnashing of teeth."

Go figure! God had allowed the lord of those

servants to see the outworking of the inworking of their individual abilities. A measure of faith has been given to every man and the anointing to multiply what he has been given, and to gain even more as you are able to handle. Use what you have and you will be given more, and that is the law of multiplication according to God!

So, God's divine order is for us to be obedient and receive life. He has set before us life and death, and it is up to us to choose. To be blessed as a result of your obedience, walk in righteousness and receive the multiplication of the commanded blessing. Which takes us right back to the beginning of what God told Adam in Genesis 1:28.

"And God blessed them, (Adam & Eve) and God said unto them, these five(5) commands:

Be fruitful (show forth my glory),

multiply (what I have given you), and

replenish (give back to what you have received of) the earth, and

subdue it (don't be afraid): and have

dominion over the fish of the sea, and over the fowl of the air, and over every living thing that moveth upon the earth."

Five is the number of Grace! God's Grace. His Grace is sufficient for you, his ability to work in you, through you and for you. So you can carry out the divine order for your life:

- *Be blessed fruitfully*
- *Be blessed to multiply*
- *Be blessed to replenish*
- *Be blessed to subdue life's circumstances*
- *Be blessed to dominate over the works of Satan*

Chapter 2

Now are We Sons

2- Now Are We Sons

Adoption

Adoption is that privilege, bestowed upon those who are united with Christ, and justified by faith, by which they are admitted into the family of God, adopted as his children, and made joint heirs with his own Son.

Although it has legal connotations, adoption is distinguished from justification.

It is also distinguished from regeneration. While regeneration refers to being spiritually reborn into the family of God, the concept of adoption refers to being included in a family one was not born into. It is essentially relational.

Through adoption, we relate to God the Father as our Father-Savior, to Jesus as our brother and co-heir and fellow sufferer, and to the Spirit as our leader and pledge (or "down payment") of our inheritance in Christ.

William E. Brown writes in Baker's Evangelical Dictionary of Biblical Theology:

"The adoption metaphor was not lost to Israel, however. God declares that he is the Father of the nation Israel, whom he loves as his child (Isa 1:2; Hosea 11:1). He tells Pharaoh, 'Israel is my firstborn son' (Exod 4:22). More specifically, he says to David (and the Messiah), "You are my son; today I have become your Father" (Psalm 2:7); and of David's descendant, "I will be his father, and he will be my son" (2 Sa 7:14). Although not precisely adoption passages, the instances of declared sonship in the Old Testament provide a theological foundation for Israel's designation as the children of God."

John 1:11-13 - Not of natural birth or the will of man, but of God. "He came to his own, and his own people did not receive him. But to all who did receive him, who believed in his name, he gave the right to become children of God, who were born, not of blood nor of the will of the flesh nor of the will of man, but of God." (ESV)

Ephesians 1:4b-6 - Believers were individually predestined for adoption

"In love he predestined us for adoption as sons through Jesus Christ, according to the purpose of his will, to the praise of his glorious grace, with which he has blessed us in the Beloved." (ESV)

Galatians 4:4-7 - Because we are sons, God has sent the Spirit of his Son into our hearts

"But when the fullness of time had come, God sent forth his Son, born of woman, born under the law, to redeem those who were under the law, so that we might receive adoption as sons. And because you are sons, God has sent the Spirit of his Son into our hearts, crying, "Abba! Father!"

So you are no longer a slave, but a son, and if a son, then an heir through God." (ESV)

Romans 8:14-23 - By the Spirit we cry, 'Abba! Father!'

"For all who are led by the Spirit of God are sons of God. For you did not receive the spirit of slavery to fall back into fear, but you have received the Spirit of adoption as sons, by whom we cry, 'Abba! Father!' The Spirit himself bears witness with our spirit that we are children of God, and if children, then heirs—heirs of God and fellow heirs with Christ, provided we suffer with him in order that we may also be glorified with him. For I consider that the sufferings of this present time are not worth comparing with the glory that is to be revealed to us. For the creation waits with eager longing for the revealing of the sons of God.

For the creation was subjected to futility, not willingly, but because of him who subjected it, in hope that the creation itself will be set free from its bondage to corruption and obtain the freedom of the glory of the children of God. For we know that the whole creation has been groaning together in the pains of childbirth until now. 23 And not only the creation, but we ourselves, who have the firstfruits of the Spirit, groan inwardly as we wait eagerly for adoption as sons, the redemption of our bodies." (ESV)

Verse 23 shows that there is "an eschatological component of adoption... The full revelation of the believer's adoption is freedom from the corruption present in the world. Being a member of God's family includes the ultimate privilege of being like him (1 Jo 3:2) and being conformed to the glorious body of Christ (Phil. 3:21). This is part of the promised inheritance for all God's children (Ro 8:16-17)."

Hebrews 12:5-11 - God disciplines every son for their good"And have you forgotten the exhortation that addresses you as sons? 'My son, do not regard lightly the discipline of the Lord, nor be weary when reproved by him. For the Lord disciplines the one he loves, and chastises every son whom he receives.' It is for discipline that you have to endure. God is treating you as sons. For what son is there whom his father does not discipline? If you are left without discipline, in which all have participated, then you are illegitimate children and not sons.

Besides this, we have had earthly fathers who disciplined us and we respected them. Shall we not much more be subject to the Father of spirits and live?

For they disciplined us for a short time as it seemed best to them, but he disciplines us for our good, that we may share his holiness. For the moment all discipline seems painful rather than pleasant, but later it yields the peaceful fruit of righteousness to those who have been trained by it." (ESV)

When we endure chastisement we move from being mere children an into sonship! When we come into the knowledge that we are sons of the Most High God we become full of passion for the things that touch God's heart! When we do this it is what the Bible calls zeal and what we generally know as passion. What is passion? It is what makes you keep going when everything is against you and others around you are throwing in the towel! It will push you to keep going to the finish line and ultimately win the race! What race are you needing to finish? Salvation is a race that we run not as others run against the each other, but against ourselves! The competition is the call to go from grace to grace and faith to faith! 23 And the very God of peace sanctify you wholly; and I pray God your whole spirit and soul and body be preserved blameless unto the coming of our Lord Jesus Christ. 24 Faithful is he that calleth you, who also will do it.

I Thesss 5:23-24 (KJV)

To endure like a good soldier and obtain the eternal reward!

Why, because Heb 10:19-23 (KJV) says, Having therefore, brethren, boldness to enter into the holiest by the blood of Jesus, 20 By a new and living way, which he hath consecrated for us, through the veil, that is to say, his flesh; 21 And having an high priest over the house of God; 22 Let us draw near with a true heart in full assurance of faith, having our hearts sprinkled from an evil conscience, and our bodies washed with pure water. **23 Let us hold fast the profession of our faith without wavering; (for he is faithful that promised;)**

It is his passion that we have received inside of us through the Gift of Eternal Life! He endured the cross for the joy that was set before him, and it was his passion to complete the work of him who had sent him!

Jesus to his disciples, those who had been disciplining in the ways of God, 32 But he said unto them, I have meat to eat that ye know not of. 33 Therefore said the disciples one to another, Hath any man brought him ought to eat? 34 Jesus saith unto them, My meat is to do the will of him that sent me, and to finish his work. John 4:32-34 (KJV) This is to be our "meat" to complete our course of salvation with passion aka zeal as obedient sons, as he was obedient to his father so that we will be numbered among the called, chosen and faithful ones upon his return!

14 These shall make war with the Lamb, and the Lamb shall overcome them: for he is Lord of lords, and King of kings: and they that are with

him are called, and chosen, and faithful. Rev 17:14 (KJV)

Chapter 3

Obey and It Will Go Well

3- Obey and It Will Go Well

Job 38:34

God, by His mighty works, convicts Job of ignorance

34 Canst thou lift up thy voice to the clouds, that abundance of waters may cover thee?

35 Canst thou send lightnings, that they may go, and say unto thee, Here we are?

36 Who hath put wisdom in the inward parts? or who hath given understanding to the heart?

Isa 47:7

7 And thou saidst, I shall be a lady for ever: so that thou didst not lay these things to thy heart, neither didst remember the latter end of it.

8 Therefore hear now this, thou that art given to pleasures, that dwellest carelessly, that sayest in

thine heart, I am, and none else beside me; I shall not sit as a widow, neither shall I know the loss of children:

9 But these two things shall come to thee in a moment in one day, the loss of children, and widowhood: they shall come upon thee in their perfection for the multitude of thy sorceries, and for the great abundance of thine enchantments.

10 For thou hast trusted in thy wickedness: thou hast said, None seeth me. Thy wisdom and thy knowledge, it hath perverted thee; and thou hast said in thine heart, I am, and none else beside me.

Isa 66:11

He comforts the humble with marvels

11 That ye may suck, and be satisfied with the breasts of her consolations; that ye may milk out, and be delighted with the abundance of her glory.

12 For thus saith the LORD, Behold, I will extend peace to her like a river, and the glory of the Gentiles like a flowing stream: then shall ye suck, ye shall be borne upon her sides, and be dandled upon her knees.

13 As one whom his mother comforteth, so will I comfort you; and ye shall be comforted in Jerusalem.

14 And when ye see this, your heart shall rejoice, and your bones shall flourish like an herb: and the hand of the LORD shall be known toward his servants, and his indignation toward his enemies.

Lk 6:45

He links the obedience of good works to the hearing of the word

45 A good man out of the good treasure of his heart bringeth forth that which is good; and an evil man out of the evil treasure of his heart

bringeth forth that which is evil: for of the abundance of the heart his mouth speaketh.

We have been given a more excellent way the Bible says a better way! That way is marking the perfect man Jesus Christ as he has completed the work by him who sent him! He suffered the pain of the cross, the death of sin that separated us from God, the burial that made him our conqueror who led captivity – captive as he entered into the bowels of hell, when he arose through the resurrection he came with all power, the keys to death, hell and the grave in his possession, and released those who were imputed as righteous from the grip of the penalty of sin! We are now the ones who are to walk as he has walked and to talk as he talked, and to face the snares of the enemy with passion aka zeal!

With determination and perserverance to let nothing separate us form the love of God! We were once headless, meaning "Ichabod" having a bend towards lawlessness and subversion to all things that were lawful! We have now been brought near who were afar off and we are now to be seated with him in heavenly places as heirs and joint-heirs. He ascended and sprinkled the blood of obedience upon the mercy seat, and in my minds' eye this is how I believe it must have sounded! The Bible says that there came a sound! That sound came on the day of pentecost and it was reported to have sounded like a rushing mighty wind according to Acts 2:2!

I believe that sound was made by the blood dropping on the mercy seat and the power and force of the blood touching the lid of the mercy seat resulted in that wind filling the upper room and when it entered into the room no one was the same!

It took on the appearance of cloven tongues "many" and resembled fire; that sanctifying fire, and they were filled with the Holy Ghost because they were obediently in one place, on one accord seeking that which Jesus had told them to wait for! It takes obedience to wait for something to happen that you have never seen or heard of before! It takes obedience to stay when others around you are ridiculing you and dissing the God you serve! It take a heart full of passion aka zeal to hold onto the exceeding and precious promises of God! No longer were they Ichabod – without a head, nothing to be subject to but themselves!

They became the chosen and royal priesthood who had become loyal subjects in the Kingdom of the Most High God! They ascended into the heavenlies without leaving earth!

Ascension Requires Submission

To enter into his gates with thanksgiving and into his courts with praise we must meet the prerequesites:

This question is asked in Who shall ascend into the hill of the LORD? or who shall stand in his holy place?

- clean hands
- pure heart
- not lifted up his soul unto vanity
- or sworn deceitfully

When they are met God says that he"...will receive the blessing from the LORD, and righteousness from the God of his salvation...this is the generation of them that seek him, that seek thy face, O Jacob. Selah." Access has now been granted!

Ephesians 2:14-18

For He Himself is our peace, who has made both one, and has broken down the middle wall of separation, having abolished in His flesh the enmity, that is, the law of commandments contained in ordinances, so as to create in

Himself one new man from the two, thus making peace, and that he might reconcile them both to God in one body through the cross, thereby putting to death the enmity. And he came and preached peace to you who were afar off and to those who were near. For through Him we both have access by one Spirit to the Father. (NKJV)

John 1:1-4, 12-14

In the beginning was the Word, and the Word was with God, and the Word was God. He was in the beginning with God. All things were made through Him, and without Him nothing was made that was made. In Him was life, and the life was the light of men. And the light shines in the darkness, and the darkness did not comprehend it…

But as many as received Him, and the world did not know Him. He came to His own, and His own did not receive Him. But as many as received

Him, to them He gave the right to become children of God, to those who believe in His name: who were born, not of blood, nor of the will of the flesh, nor of the will of man, but of God. And the Word became flesh and dwelt among us, and we beheld His glory, the glory as of the only begotten of the Father, full of grace and truth.

Hebrews 12:5-29

And you have forgotten the exhortation which speaks to you as to sons: My son, do not despise the chastening of the Lord, Nor be discouraged when you are rebuked by Him; For whom the Lord loves He chastens, And scourges every son whom He receives. If you endure chastening, God deals with you as with sons, for what son is there whom a father does not chasten? But if you are without chastening, of which all have become partakers, then you are illegitimate and not sons. We have had human fathers who corrected us, and we paid them respect. Shall we not much more readily be in subjection to the Father of the spirits and live? For they indeed for a few days chastened us as seemed best to them, but he for our profit, that we may be partakers of His holiness. Now no chastening seems to be joyful for the present, but painful, nevertheless, afterward it yields the peaceable fruit of righteousness to those who have been trained by it.

Therefore strengthen the hands which hang down, and the feeble knees, and make straight paths for your feet, so that what is lame may not be dislocated, but rather be healed. Pursue peace with all people, and holiness, without which no one will see the Lord: looking carefully lest anyone fall short of the grace of God; lest any root of bitterness springing up cause trouble, and by this many become defiled; lest there be any fornicator or profane person like Esau, who for one morsel of food sold his birthright.

For you know that afterward, when we wanted to inherit the blessing, he was rejected, for he found no place for repentance, though he sought it diligently with tears. For you have not come to the mountain that may be touched and that burned with fire, and to blackness and darkness and tempest, and the sound of a trumpet and the voice of words, so that those who heard it begged that the word should not be spoken to them anymore. (For they could not endure what was commanded: And if so much as a beast touches the mountain, it shall be stoned or shot with an arrow." And so terrifying was the sight that Moses said, "I am exceedingly afraid and trembling.")

But you have come to Mount Zion and to the city of the living God, the heavenly Jerusalem, to an innumerable company of angels, to the general assembly and church of the firstborn who are registered in heaven, to God the Judge of all, to the spirits of just men made perfect, to Jesus the Mediator of the new covenant, and the blood of sprinkling speaks better things than that of Abel.

See that you do not refuse Him who speaks. For if they did not escape who refused Him who spoke on earth, much more shall we not escape if we turn away from Him who speaks from heaven, whose voice then shook the earth, but now He has promised, saying, "Yet once more I shake not only the earth, but also heaven." Now this, yet once more, "indicates the removal of those things that are being shaken, as of things that are made, that the things which cannot be shaken may remain. Therefore, since we are receiving a kingdom that cannot be shaken, let us have grace, by which we serve God acceptably with reverence and godly fear. For our God is a consuming fire.

Galatians 4:1-11

Now I say that the heir as long as he is a child, does not differ at all from a slave, though he is master of all, but his guardians and stewards until the time appointed by the father. Even so we, when we were children, were in bondage under the elements of the world.

When we were once in bondage under the elements of the world. But when the fullness of time had come, God sent forth His Son, born of a woman, born under the law, to redeem those who were under the law, that we might receive the adoption as sons. And because you are sons, God has sent forth the Spirit of His Son into your hearts, crying out, "Abba, Father!' Therefore you are no longer a slave but a son, and if a son, then an heir of God through Christ. But then, indeed, when you did not know God, you served those that by nature are not gods. But now after you have known God, or rather are known by God, how is it that you turn again to the weak and beggarly elements, to which you desire again to be in bondage? You observe days and months and seasons and years. I am afraid for you, lest I have labored for you in vain.

Romans 10:3

For they being ignorant of God's righteousness, and seeking to establish their own righteousness, has not submitted to the righteousness of God. Christ is the end of the law for righteousness to everyone who believes. For Moses wrote about the righteousness which is of the law, "The man who does those things shall live by them." But the righteousness of faith speaks in this way, "Do not say in your heart, "…who will ascend into heaven?" (That is, to bring Christ down from above) or, "who will descend into the abyss?" (That is, to bring Christ up from the dead). But what does it say? "The word is near you, in your mouth and in your heart" (that is, the word of faith which we preach): that if you confess with your mouth the Lord Jesus and believe in your heart that God raised Him from the dead, you **will be saved**.

For with the heart one believes, has relationship unto righteousness, and with the mouth confession is made unto salvation. For the Scripture says, "Whoever believes on Him will not be put to shame. For there is no distinction between the Jew and Greek, for the same Lord over all is rich to all who call upon Him. For "whoever calls on the name of the Lord shall be saved."

James 4:1-10

Where do wars and fights come from among you? Do they not come from your desires for pleasure that war in your members? You lust and do not have. You murder and covet and cannot obtain. You fight and war. Yet you do not have because you do not ask. You ask and do not receive, because you ask amiss, that you may spend it on pleasures.

Adulterers and adulteresses! Do you not know that friendship with the world is enmity with God? Whoever therefore wants to be a friend of the world makes himself an enemy of God. Or do you think that the Scripture says in vain, "The Spirit who dwells in us yearns jealously"? But He gives more grace, Therefore He says: "God resist the proud, But gives grace to the humble." Therefore submit to God. Resist the devil and he will flee from you.

Draw near to God and He will draw near to you. Cleanse your hands, you sinners; and purify your hearts, you doubleminded.

Lament and mourn and weep! Let your laughter be turned to mourning and your joy to gloom. Humble yourselves in the sight of the Lord, and

He will lift you up.

Satan's anointing rode us like a wet blanket before salvation. As an anointed cherub in heaven, he had God's holy anointing. His anointing has been perverted, polluted and empowered by the works of the flesh. This is why Satan accuses us with our past, because it is his past that keeps him locked into the position of defeat by God. Our defeat fuels his passion and power!

God commands us to forget those things which are behind so that his anointing keeps us victorious and in relationship.

My Father and I are one! It is the self-same anointing in us that quickened Christ from the dead! I recall one year a portion of a radio broadcast quoting an interview given to a world wide news media on a celebrity. In the article this celebrity spoke of how they hated themselves. I was dressing for work, and God began to reveal to me why Satan has a grip on suicide as a tool to destroy lives. He has perverted the truth. If any man would follow me, let him deny himself. To die is gain…I die daily…It is no longer I that lives but, Christ that lives in me…I in him, I move, live and have my being…all things exist in him and through him.

When an individual is despairing of himself, he feels the only answer is to be free of him self.

So to do this he must kill his body and cease to be an issue or source of pain to himself or others. This is a signal that there is a need for freedom, but the answer eludes the natural mind. How?

Satan uses his tools of perversion to cloud the mind. But the answer that disperses the cloud of confusion is a true and personal relationship with Jesus Christ.

All of the other volumes of the books of the Bible have been to bring you to this point and that you have seen the diasporas of life through the word of God. We are now into maintaining your freedom. To do this requires a relationship with one who is able to relate to us as we are, right where we are, right when we need him. All we have to do is reach out to Him with these words "Come into my heart any make me over in your image."

A new life and identity just like Gideon.' His name meant to be "cut down." A surrendering of the heart is what is done in the hidden part. To rend the garment and not the heart is a form of pride and an outward show of self. God requires us to make a private place for him, so that he can demonstrate as he chooses, when he chooses. This is liberty that moves in God as we are drawn into his presence.

Drawing nigh to God will bring us into Jubilee. Released from the debts of the past years the fulfillment of the covenant (manifesting) the evidence of life whose debts have been cancelled.

We proclaim (prophesy) it and He "God" will establish it.

God said that he hastens to perform his word. Through that performance a supernatural unity is created and the favor of the Lord enshrouds us.

Surrounds as the mountains surround Jerusalem, so the Lord surrounds his people with the kind of favor that releases us from prison. Pushes us back into the posture of what God originally designed or us before Adam's fall. All or our senses become new: ears, eyes and vocals – to hear, see and speak as he directs. Senses that alert to and recognize the voice of the good shepherd.

Running to be in his presence, and stand strong in the anointing. Strong in the Hebrew is Astam; meaning in body in Psalms 139:14 –

Al Novak, states in Hebrew Honey, "That is, the human body which is wonderfully made and is composed of a million projects bound together." As we abide in the presence of the Holy of Holies we are sustained, established, planted and firm in our places. The more we worship the Holy One, the more we become God conscious instead of sin conscious. This revelation produces Jubilee. With our senses heightened to be on cue to hearken (hear and obey) our supernatural strength allows us to know things before they happen; even too while they are happening.

There is a pattern to be taken notice of here – As our sin debts have been supernaturally cancelled, we too must supernaturally cancel the sin debts that others owe us.

Injuries to our emotional, physical, and financial health. Understand I am speaking of forgiveness. Many will never be able to pay you back for emotional, and physical pain.

Once you have been injured a scar occurs in its place. It requires the salve of forgiveness to penetrate beneath the scabs and bruises to bring true healing. Even financially, you may sue or get repaid, but the strain of the loss is felt long after.

God has painted us with the anointed fragrance of the undefiled blood of his son in Luke 4, and God is attracted to the sweet smell of sacrifice. He in turn is compelled to pour out his free favor on us. This blood is whole; it does not carry the illnesses of the curse. Therefore, there is no stench. Unlike the blood of animals and man, that carries the stench of active curses. That blood carries an obtrusive odor. The components are entangled with the components of death; sickness and disease.

Jesus has shown himself strong on our behalf, bringing us out of the stench of death and obscurity. It is like 'Honey in the Rock" – the revelation knowledge revealed through Jesus, His Blood, His Anointing and His Word.

Jesus has become our way of escape, our door out of the land of Egypt, and our compass through the wilderness, and our securer of the promises in the Promise Land. In I Corinthians 10:11-13, it is stated "Now all these things happened unto them for ensamples: and they are written for our admonition, upon whom the ends of the world are come. Wherefore let him that thinketh that he standeth take heed lest he fall. There hath no temptation taken you but such as is common to man: but God is faithful, who will not suffer you to be tempted above that ye are able, but will with the temptation also make a way to escape, that ye may be able to bear it."

All of our problems must be faced with the knowledge that where the Son is there is Liberty through his anointing. No matter what we face, God through his Son Jesus has been broken the authority of it for us. We simply have to receive and work the authority that has been given us over death, hell and the grave through intimate love with the triune personhood of God.

Beth Moore, in "Things Pondered" expounds on I Corinthians 13:8. "Love never fails"…"Does it never fail the giver or the receiver?" It fails neither. For the receiver they will never have been loved for nothing. God is very practical.

If he has called upon you to be His vessel of love toward someone else it is because He has a plan … Love never fails the Giver … He never "fails" to make the unlovely lovely to you … There will be times that it will break our hearts to be vessels of God's love toward another, but its ultimate end is meant for salvation. The salvation of someone's soul, health, reputation, marriage, honor, sanity. Through love He saves spirit, soul, mind and body"

We must first present our bodies as a living sacrifice, no longer a need to die the death of the cross for our sins. He has taken our place, but not removed the responsibility of offering ourselves as offerings in the use of kingdom business. We are to be with clean hands and a pure heart, have your hands shed innocent blood or served with ulterior motives? Clean your hands through the washing of the water of the word; apply the word of God to the sins committed by the hands. Purify your heart with the fire of the word through the refiners fire and the habitation of the Holy Spirit pressing out the old man and writing the heart of God into your heart! Repent of seeking the hand of God above the face of God and of any means by which you have decieved yourself or others.

Chapter 4

Give Me Something To Pour Into

4- Give Me Something to Pour Into

Jesus was a vessel prepared by God to take away the sins of the world and to lead captivity captive!

Hebrews 10:4-9, "4 For *it is* not possible that the blood of bulls and of goats should take away sins. 5 Wherefore when he cometh into the world, he saith, Sacrifice and offering thou wouldest not, but a body hast thou prepared me: 6 In burnt offerings and *sacrifices* for sin thou hast had no pleasure. 7 Then said I, Lo, I come (in the volume of the book it is written of me,) to do thy will, O God. 8 Above when he said, Sacrifice and offering and burnt offerings and *offering* for sin thou wouldest not, neither hadst pleasure *therein*; which are offered by the law; 9 Then said he, Lo, I come to do thy will, O God. He taketh away the first, that he may establish the second."

We are the vessels that have been begotten through his laying down his life in the soil of sin and being crushed by death and conquering death, hell and the grave through his descent into the depths of hell and getting up with all power in his hands. Having the keys to death hell and the grave and leading captivity captive and releasing the righteous from the grips of Satan and ascending as our final High Priest and sprinkled the blood on the mercy seat that was no longer comminged, but pure and undefiled! We are his harvest because he was planted as a son and he reaped after his own kind! He has given us the right to become sons and heirs of promise through that one amazing key!

We are vessels after the manner in which his father prepared him to redeem us back to his father! We are children of God by birthright and sons of God through obedience!

In today's society provides mass production of almost everything. Our toys, cars, computers and even food are mass produced, yet Advertisers invite us to be different by buying special clothes, shoes and automobiles which are all mass produced!

Are we all alike or are we different? We are all the same in birthright, true! But not all the same in sonship, because not all children are obedient children!

Much of mankind rebels against the things that are really different. We have seen the cruelty of children to another who dresses differently. We start a new job with enthusiasm and drive and soon co-workers are sizing you up and determining whether you fit in with any of their groups. Some will suggest that you relax and join the group and become like everyone else. Yet, we are not to be like everyone else because we have not been mass produced. The supreme Creator has made it possible for each of us to be unique through his perfect plan. We are not clones or carbon copies. He is the ultimate potter.

Still, we do not have a good comprehension of the potter's work today. Up until the development of pottery, mankind was nomadic. He had to follow the game for food or follow a stream. To be near water. Can you imagine what our lives would be like without containers?

With vessels things changed, we could carry food and water around, Settlements developed.

The potter became a major influence in society and people gathered at his shop to see the new vessels and purchase those needed.

 You see each vessel was unique. Each had something special to recommend it to its purpose. We all know of the works of Jeremiah. Through out his sixty odd years he faced much adversity. His life spoke louder than his words, at one point in his life he showed vulnerability, his discouragement.

Let's look at chapter Jeremiah 12: 1 – 6

1   Righteous are You, O LORD, when I plead with You; Yet let me talk with You about Your judgments. Why does the way of the wicked prosper? Why are those happy who deal so treacherously? 2 You have planted them, yes, they have taken root; They grow, yes, they bear fruit. You are near in their mouth But far from their mind. 3   But You, O LORD, know me; You have seen me, And You have tested my heart toward You. Pull them out like sheep for the slaughter, And prepare them for the day of slaughter. 4   How long will the land mourn, And the herbs of every field wither? The beasts and birds are consumed, For the wickedness of those who dwell there, Because they said, "He will not see our final end." 5   "If you have run with the footmen, and they have wearied you, Then how

can you contend with horses? And if in the land of peace, In which you trusted, they wearied you…

6   For even your brothers, the house of your father, Even they have dealt treacherously with you; Yes, they have called a multitude after you. Do not believe them, Even though they speak smooth words to you.

Jeremiah is frustrated, discouraged and confused at what is happening. BUT He later says "I will run and I will endure."

Throughout his ministry "endurance" is his cry God tells Jeremiah to go down to the potter's house.

Jeremiah18: 1 – 10:

God is the potter. He is willing to clean up the mess Israel has made. He wants vessels of endurance. Vessels that can take the heat without cracking. He wants you to be a chosen vessel of His. Jeremiah understood the concept of the potter as did Israel. Isaiah used some of the same concepts in his writings.

II Chronicles 24:12 says, "whereof were made vessels for the house of the Lord, even vessels to minister and to offer…"

Each vessel has a two-fold purpose:

1) to minister meaning "to serve"

Focuses on horizontal dimension of our lives and We serve one another in love in order that we may

2) offer meaning to "cause to go up" Focuses on the vertical dimension.

Our relationship with GOD. We cause our praises and thanksgiving to go up to Him as vessels offering a sacrificial praise! We are to be vessels of offering to God. We are called both to serve and to worship, yet again in II Corinthians 4:7, "But we have this treasure in earthen vessels, that the excellency of the power may be of God, and not of us." Let's look at the Greek word for "the excellency of the power" in this verse. The Greek word means "to exceed the mark, to stretch a truth."

So, our earthen vessels contain a treasure of Spirit-filled excess.

Looking now into I Thessalonians 4:3-4 "For this is the will of God, even your sanctification, that you should abstain from fornication: that every one of you should know how to possess his vessel in sanctification and honor."

Note it is our responsibility to possess our vessels in in sanctification and honor!

We have a part to play in our usability.

Jeremiah's metaphors were choice and filled with life as he cried, "Come back to the potter's care. He will make you into another vessel."

So we have vessels, each of which is carefully made by the Potter's hand. They are vessels for pouring out to God and others. Vessels filled with treasure in excess. We are common clay jars that have been anointed for God's service and We are encouraged to keep these vessels in sanctification and honor. What an awesome privilege to be formed and used by the Creator of the universe for the purpose of bearing His name.

After the Potter's touch, we can never be the same. Even to us God is saying, "Go down to the potter's house and there I will speak to you." He tells us to go to the Potter's House to gain wisdom and insight which will lead and guide us into the way of holiness!

Sometimes we become tired and frustrated and begin to drift off course. The Holy Spirit has now become our navigational system that if we will only asks for help he will lead and guide us into all truth! Should we fail to ask for help and we drift off course the Holy Spirit will automatically correct us and it is up to us to yield to the correction or continue on the same path of error! The Holy Spirit is not afraid to shake us, to awaken us or correct our direction! He resides in us until we get off course, he cannot dwell in an unclean temple when we are off course. Most of us remember the song of a few years ago which said, "He touched Me, Oh He touched me. And oh the joy that filled my soul." Job found no immediate joy in God's touch: "Have pity on me, have pity on me, O ye my friends; for the hand of God has touched me." It's OK to feel the touch of God's hand – good or bad. We should desire the gentle pressure of the Potter's hand.

The clay must yield to His touch. For the believer there is really no choice. Through the Potter's touch may feel violent as change takes place, be assured that the Potter knows what He is doing. You are in good hands – so relax – rest – grow. God wants you to be what He desires – strong – usable – beautiful – yielded. As the potter sits at the wheel, he starts with throwing a lump of clay on the wheel.

And the clay is not pliable at first, it must be subjected to the process of being prepared to be molded into the vision of the potter! So many times we ask God why has he made us the way he made us and given us the temptations, trials and tests that he has given us! But without the temptation, trials or tests we would not know that our vessel was capable of completing the purpose for which is was created! We have all been given a purpose, but many times we don't know what that purpose is!

Clearly Jeremiah, says this about purpose for the obedient!

11 For I know the thoughts that I think toward you, saith the LORD, thoughts of peace, and not of evil, to give you an expected end. 12 Then shall ye call upon me, and ye shall go and pray unto me, and I will hearken unto you. 13 And ye shall seek me, and find me, when ye shall search for me with all your heart. 14 And I will be found of you, saith the LORD: and I will turn away your captivity, and I will gather you from all the nations, and from all the places whither I have driven you, saith the LORD; and I will bring you again into the place whence I caused you to be carried away captive. Jer 29:11-14 (KJV)

It is in this passage that we find that our purpose should be in following the plan of God for our lives, and where might this plan be found? In his written word the Bible and in relationship with him!

When we are no longer strangers he begins to share his plans with us and as we mature in our relationship he begins to tell us more, and as we become pliable and less resistant we become servants and then we move from servants to friends. Friends are told mysteries and not just plans!

Chapter 5

The Plan of Salvation

5- The Plan of Salvation

"By this it is evident who are the children of God, and who are the children of the devil: whoever does not practice righteousness is not of God, nor is the one who does not love his brother." (1 John 3:10, ESV)

Lordship salvation is the position that receiving Christ involves a turning in the heart from sin and, as a part of faith, a submissive commitment to obey Jesus Christ as Lord. It also maintains that progressive sanctification and perseverance must necessarily follow conversion. Those who hold to the doctrine of perseverance of the saints see this not only as a requirement, but an assured certainty according to the sustaining grace of Christ.

The doctrine of lordship salvation has implications for evangelism, assurance, and the pursuit of holiness. The grace of God in salvation not only forgives, but transforms, and a lack of obedience or transformation in a person's life is warrant to doubt that they have been born again. The grounds for assurance include not only the objective promises of God (like John 3:16), but also the internal testimony of the Spirit (Romans 8:16) and holiness the Spirit produces in our lives (1 John 2:3-4,19).

The non-lordship salvation position is popularly known by critics as "easy believism", and by adherents as "free grace". However, proponents of Lordship salvation frown upon this usage of the term "free grace", as the free grace spoken of the Bible both justifies the sinner and transforms the heart unto obedience.

Receiving Jesus Christ in repentance and faith

There is a close relationship between that of receiving Christ and having faith in Christ. In fact, the two are indistinguishable. There cannot be an individual who has truly received Christ who lacks faith in Christ, or an individual who has faith in Christ but has yet to receive him.

"We can do nothing but only receive Christ and what he has done already. Salvation is not offered to us upon any condition, but freely and for nothing. We are to do nothing for it; we are only to take it. This taking and receiving is faith. ... Faith cannot be called the condition of receiving, for it is the receiving itself." (Jonathan Edwards) It is the gift of God

The apostle Paul writes explaining the way in which believers begin with Christ: in faith with thanksgiving. He encourages the Colossians to continue in the same way that they began or received Christ.

"Therefore, as you received Christ Jesus the Lord, so walk in him, rooted and built up in him and established in the faith, just as you were taught, abounding in thanksgiving." (Col 2:6-7)

Saving faith "energizes a life of love and obedience"

Sam Storms writes:

"The doctrine of Lordship Salvation views saving faith neither as passive nor fruitless. The faith that is the product of regeneration, the faith that embraces the atoning sacrifice of Jesus on the cross energizes a life of love and obedience and worship. The controversy is not a dispute about whether salvation is by faith only or by faith plus works. All agree that we are saved by grace through faith, apart from works (Eph. 2:8-10). But the controversy is about the nature of the faith that saves."

Repentance is a turning in the heart from sin to God. Jesus evangelistically calls people to discipleship

When Jesus preached the gospel, he both called men to trust in his promises and to follow him in radical discipleship. Among Christians there is no elite subcategory of joint-heirs with Christ

Paul writes in Romans 8:16-17:

"The Spirit himself bears witness with our spirit that we are children of God, and if children, then heirs—heirs of God and fellow heirs with Christ, provided we suffer with him in order that we may also be glorified with him."

Richard P. Belcher writes,

"The Greek word in Romans 8:17 speaks of glorification and not reigning. It is a word related to the one translated 'glorified' in [Romans 8:30]. The word in verse 17 is a compound verb (a prepositional prefix with a simple verb), while the word in verse 30 is the simple verb alone... Clearly both a simple reading of the passage and a careful interpretation of the passage brings us to the same conclusion. We are heirs---join-heir with God in Christ. The reality of our relation to Christ is shown in our lives of suffering for Him, and we shall be glorified together with Him."

That Paul is not dividing his audience into two kinds of justified Christians---inheritors and non-inheritors---is made apparent by the very next verse (11):

"And such were some of you. But you were washed, you were sanctified, you were justified in the name of the Lord Jesus Christ and by the Spirit of our God."

Concerning Matthew 25:31-46, he goes to write,

"In [this passage], Jesus is describing what will happen when He returns to this earth in glory and sits on His glorious throne (v. 31). At this time, He will gather the nations before Him and separate humanity into two groups of people (v. 32), placing the sheep on His right and the goats on His left (v. 33). The sheep, of course, represent believers (vv. 34-40) and the goats represent unbelievers (vv. 41-45).

Later, Jesus describes how He will tell the goats: 'Depart from Me, accursed ones, into the eternal fire which has been prepared for the devil and his angels' (v. 41). But first He addresses the sheep, saying to them: 'Come, you who are blessed of My Father, inherit the kingdom prepared for you from the foundation of the world' (v. 34; emphasis added). All believers, Jesus says, will inherit the kingdom.

"According to the [non-lordship] view, Jesus should have divided humanity into three groups: (1) the righteous sheep who will inherit the kingdom, (2) the unrighteous sheep who will enter but not inherit the kingdom, and (3) the unrighteous goats who will depart into eternal fire. But instead, He divided them into two (and only two) groups of people: (1) the sheep who will inherit the kingdom and (2) the goats who will go away into eternal punishment. These two groups are otherwise known as the blessed ones and accursed ones (vv. 34, 41), the righteous and the unrighteous (v. 46). Again, all true believers will inherit the kingdom of God."

A person can be saved and not know fully the implications of Christ's lordship.

John Piper writes:

"[S]omething may be real even when we don't understand it fully or even use the right language to describe it. For example, is a person not 'born again' just because he has never heard the term 'born again' and does not relate to Jesus in those terms but only in terms of faith and forgiveness and atonement? No. A person is just as born again if he believes in Jesus, even if he has never heard of the word 'regeneration' or the term 'born again'. Many have been born again and saved through gospel tracts which say nothing about the term 'rebirth.' ... [N]one of us yet understands the full implications of the lordship of Christ on our lives. I am struggling every day to know what the Lord is requiring of me in specific choices among good options. I am learning every day the extent of his lordly control of the world and his mysterious ways of fulfilling his promises as Lord of my life and my church.

Submitting to the lordship of Christ is a lifelong activity. It must be renewed every day in many acts of trust and obedience. Submission to Christ's lordship is not merely a once-for-all experience."[5]

Our submission to Christ is imperfect and progressive due in part to some unhelpful rhetoric by proponents of lordship salvation, some have objected that it "places sanctification before salvation. If people are to give up/turn from all of their sins before they are saved, then, in essence, they are to become sanctified before they are saved. This is something that no Christian has achieved in this life—not even Paul could claim such an achievement at the end of his life (Phil. 3:12)."

Salvation should be distinguished from discipleship. "This Lordship teaching fails to distinguish salvation from discipleship and makes requirements for discipleship prerequisites for salvation. Our Lord distinguished the two (Luke 14:16-33). This teaching elevates one of the many aspects of the person of Christ (Master over life) in making it a part of the Gospel. Why not require faith in His kingship? Or in the fact that He is Judge of all, or that He was the Creator? Though my view has been dubbed "easy believism," it is not easy to believe, because what we ask the unsaved person to believe in not easy. We ask that he trust a person who lived two thousand years ago, whom he can only know through the Bible, to forgive his sins. We are asking that he stake his eternal destiny on this.

Remember the example of Evangelist; Jesus. He did not require the Samaritan woman to set her sinful life in order, or even be willing to, so that she could be saved. He did not set out before her what would be expected by way of changes in her life if she believed.

He simply said she needed to know who He is and to ask for the gift of eternal life (John 4:10)." - Charles Ryrie, Basic Theology.

"But how can we be sure that we have really believed? Therein lies a problem created by traditions, not by the Word of God. That question is foreign to the biblical gospel. There is no such thing as true faith as opposed to false faith. All faith is faith. If we believe in Christ for eternal life, then we have eternal life and we know we have it, because He guarantees it, 'He who believes in Me has everlasting life' (John 6:47). This notion directly contradicts James 2, which distinguishes living and dead faith: "So also faith by itself, if it does not have works, is dead." - James 2:17

Paul likewise speaks of a "vain" faith, which is manifested when one does not "hold fast to the word":

"Now I would remind you, brothers, of the gospel I preached to you, which you received, in which you stand, and by which you are being saved, if you hold fast to the word I preached to you-- unless you believed in vain." - 1 Corinthians 15:1-

Yet, there is a process by which salvation is fully realized in the life of the one who has chosen to believe on the Lord Jesus Christ and be saved!

Chapter 6
The Process
Of
Salvation

6- The Process of Salvation

I Thesssalonians Chapter 5

I Thesssalonians 5:1

5:1 But of the times and the seasons, brethren, ye have no need that I write unto you.

The day that God has appointed for this judgment we do not know. But this is sure, that it will come upon men when they are not expecting it.

I Thessalonians 5:4

But ye, brethren, are not in darkness, that that day should overtake you as a thief. Returning to exhortations, he warns us who are enlightened with the knowledge of God, that it is our duty not to live securely in pleasures, lest we be suddenly taken in a dead sleep in pleasures. But contrary to this we are to have an eye to the Lord, and not allow ourselves to be oppressed with the cares of this world, for pleasures are fitting for the darkness of the night, and having an eye to the Lord is fitting for the light.

I Thessalonians 5:8

5:8 But let us, who are of the day, be sober, putting on the breastplate of faith and love; and for an helmet, the hope of salvation.

We must fight with faith and hope, and therefore we should certainly not lie snoring.

I Thessalonians 5:9

5:9 For God hath not appointed us to wrath, but to obtain salvation by our Lord Jesus Christ,

He urges us forward by setting a most certain hope of victory before us.

I Thessalonians 5:10

5:10 Who died for us, that, whether we wake or sleep, we should live together with him.

The death of Christ is a pledge of our victory, for he died so that we might be partakers of his life of power, indeed even while we live here.

I Thesssalonians 5:11

5:11 Wherefore comfort yourselves together, and edify one another, even as also ye do.

We must not only watch ourselves, but we are also bound to stir up, and to strengthen and encourage one another.

I Thesssalonians 5:12

5:12 And we beseech you, brethren, to know them which labour among you, and are over you in the Lord, and admonish you; We must have consideration of those who are appointed to the ministry of the word, and the government of the church of God, and who do their duty.

That you acknowledge and take them for such as they are, that is to say, men worthy to be greatly esteemed of among you.

In those things which pertain to God's service: so is the ecclesiastical function distinguished from civil authority, and true shepherds from wolves.

I Thesssalonians 5:13

5:13 And to esteem them very highly in love for their work's sake. [And] be at peace among yourselves.

So then, when this reason ceases, then must the honour cease.

The maintenance of mutual harmony, is to be especially guarded.

I Thesssalonians 5:14

5:14 Now we exhort you, brethren, warn them that are unruly, comfort the feebleminded, support the weak, be patient toward all [men].

We must have consideration of every man, and the remedy must be applied according to the disease. That keep not their rank or standing.

I Thesssalonians 5:15

5:15 See that none render evil for evil unto any [man]; but ever follow that which is good, both among yourselves, and to all [men].

Charity ought not to be overcome by any injuries.

I Thesssalonians 5:16

5:16 Rejoice evermore.

A quiet and appeased mind is nourished with continual prayers, giving regard to the will of God.

I Thesssalonians 5:18

5:18 In every thing give thanks: for this is the will of God in Christ Jesus concerning you.

An acceptable thing to God, and such as he approves well of.

I Thesssalonians 5:19

5:19 Quench not the Spirit.

Geneva Study Notes - I Thesssalonians 5

The sparks of the Spirit of God that are kindled in us, are nourished by daily hearing the word of God: but true doctrine must be diligently distinguished from false.

I Thesssalonians 5:20

5:20 Despise not prophesyings.

The explaining and interpreting of the word of God.

I Thesssalonians 5:22

5:22 Abstain from all appearance of evil.

A general conclusion, that we waiting for the coming of Christ, do give ourselves to pureness in mind, will, and body, through the grace and strength of the Spirit of God. Whatever has but the very show of evil, abstain from it.

I Thesssalonians 5:23

5:23 And the very God of peace sanctify you wholly; and [I pray God] your whole spirit and soul and body be preserved blameless unto the coming of our Lord Jesus Christ.

Separate you from the world, and make you holy to himself through his Spirit, in Christ, in whom alone you will attain to that true peace.

I Thesssalonians 5:24

5:24 Faithful [is] he that calleth you, who also

will do [it]. The good will and power of God is a sure strengthening and encouragement against all difficulties, of which we have a sure witness in our calling.

Always one, and ever like himself, who indeed performs whatever he promises. And an effectual calling is nothing else but a right declaring and true setting forth of God's will: and therefore the salvation of the elect, is safe and sure.

Who will also make you perfect.

I Thesssalonians 5:25

5:25 Brethren, pray for us.

The last part of the epistle, in which with most authoritative charge he commends both himself and this epistle to them.

Salvations Ladder

The ladder of Salvation begins at the bottom Step at propitiation and ascends to the top step of glorification and the sprinkling of the blood on the Mercy Seat – sealed our access to Salvation. Matthew 25:33-34 says that, "31 When the Son of man shall come in his glory, and all the holy angels with him, then shall he sit upon the throne of his glory: 32 And before him shall be gathered all nations: and he shall separate them one from another, as a shepherd divideth his sheep from the goats: 33 And he shall set the sheep on his right hand, but the goats on the left.

34 Then shall the King say unto them on his right hand, Come, ye blessed of my Father, inherit the kingdom prepared for you from the foundation of the world: ..."

Through 42 generations he came and passed the test so that all men might be saved if only they would believe! The numbers of each step correlate to the biblical number significances.

Biblical Numbers Significance

Step 1 New beginning

Step 2 Union

Step 3 Divine perfection

Step 4 Creation, works

Step 5 Grace, 5 books

Step 6 Mans Weakness

Step 7 Resurrection; Spiritual completeness; Fathers perfection

Step 8 New birth; new beginnings

Step 9 Fruit of the spirit; Divine completeness

Step 10 Testimony; Law and responsibility

Step 11 Disorder and judgment

Step 12 Governmental perfection

Step 13 speaks of Apostasy; depravity/rebellion

Step 14 Deliverance; Salvation

Through salvation we obtain rest, because he worked the work of him that sent him so we would not.

Our works were insufficient to satisfy God, but his work was sufficient in all manners and now God has been satisfied! The debt has been paid and we are no longer debtors to sin, but free to be lead in the spiritual perfection that is freely poured out even now!

Step 1 Propitiation

To be "ONE" is to be united and untied from the source according to the word "Echad" in the Hebrew. As we are no longer debtors owing a debt we could never pay but ransomed through the payment that satisfied God through the substitutionary death of his son Jesus Christ. He became our propitiation!

The word propitiation carries the basic idea of

appeasement, or satisfaction, specifically towards God. Propitiation is a two-part act that involves appeasing the wrath of an offended person and being reconciled to them."

Propitiation is that "by which it becomes consistent with his character and government to pardon and bless the sinner. The propitiation does not procure his love or make him loving; it only renders it consistent for him to exercise his love towards sinners." In Rom. 3:25 and Heb. 9:5 the Greek word hilasterion (KJV, "mercy-seat") is used. The Hebrew kapporeth, which means "covering," is used of the lid of the ark of the covenant (Ex. 25:21; 30:6). Hilasterion came to mean the mercy-seat or lid of the ark, and the propitiation or reconciliation by blood.

In speaking with a messianic jew they explained to me that an unknown about the bucket of blood is that oftentimes the blood of bullocks and goats was also commingled with the blood of the circumcision! They also spoke of the bloody mess the temple was in because of all day long the sacrifices were being made. The imagery we have in our mind is of the clean and golden pictures we see presented to us! But the blood was being offered in buckets for the entire nation of Israel! It was a bloody mess!

On the great day of atonement "Yom Kippur" it was a time of mourning when the high priest carried the blood of the sacrifice he offered for all the people within the veil and sprinkled it on the "mercy-seat," and so made propitiation.

In 1 John 2:2; 4:10, Christ is called the "propitiation for our sins." Here a different Greek word is used, hilasmos. Christ is "the propitiation," because by his becoming our substitute and assuming our obligations he expiated our guilt, covering it by the vicarious punishment which he endured.

Propitiation versus Expiation

Propitiation made it possible for the sin debt to be satisfied that God required once and for all.

Expiation meant that the cleansing of our sins appeased God's anger.

The death of our savior made him the solution to the problem of sin and we were one afar from God have been made near to him through the sacrifice of the paschal lamb.

Step 2 - Redemption

1. An act of redeeming or the state of being redeemed.
2. Deliverance; rescue.
3. Theology. Deliverance from sin; salvation.
4. Atonement for guilt.
5. Repurchase, as of something sold.

Redemption released us from the captivity of sin and set the captives free because the ransom has been paid. As the Israelites were redeemed from

Egypt so we are redeemed from the power of sin and the curse of the Law through Jesus.

We have been bought with a price and we are no longer our own and we should seek him with our whole hearts!

We are the righteousness of God in Christ Jesus! We have been wrapped in the robe of many colors of Joseph which signifies we are now favored sons of God! The place of his crucifixion was on a place called Golgotha "skull" in my mind I envision this as his cross being impaled in the center of the head of the mind of evil and as he was hanging on the cross the blood was streaming down and flowing into the opening of the ground of the skull and causing it to tremble because it was under going a mind shaking experience! Before on the place of the skull only the guilty were hung there and their blood streamed down and into the opening of the skull and only increased its position of an evil mind!

But when the innocent blood of the second Abel whose blood was also innocent and cried out for justice!

At that moment justice was being applied to all of those who had died with righteousness imputed unto them but had been held in hell!

The place of the skull that day had three crosses impaled inside of it and the one that was on the center cross was innocent between two who were guilty reconciling the sins of the world! One would join him in His kingdom and the other would join Satan in hell!

Calvary, in other words, not merely made possible the salvation of those for whom Christ died; it ensured that they would be brought to faith and their salvation be made actual.

Step 3 - Reconciliation

As stated above, Jesus' death satisfied and

reconciled sinners to God. Yet, in order to fully appreciate the doctrine of the atonement it must be made clear why the atonement was necessary.

Let's look at two theories on reconciliation:

The Ransom Theory:

"The earliest of all, originating with the Early Church Fathers, this theory claims that Christ offered himself as a ransom (Mark 10:45). Where it was not clear was in its understanding of exactly to whom the ransom was paid. Many early church fathers viewed the ransom as paid to Satan."

Step 4 - Election

Election refers to God's choosing of individuals or peoples to be the objects of his grace or to otherwise fulfill his purposes. Most often God's election is Election and predestination are very similar concepts to the point that the terms can sometimes be used interchangeably. However, there is a difference in the emphasis of the two terms.

Election primarily has in view God's sovereign selection, whereas predestination accents the purpose or goal of His election.

Scripture clearly teaches both election and predestination; however, there are a variety of views as to who, when, why, and how God does so.

This election is freely offered to all. Anyone who wants to be identified with Christ, becomes part of the elect, and is assured of salvation. But at the same time they can lose that salvation if they cease to be identified with Christ.

An analogy used is that, Christ is the captain of a ship called "elect" (which is the Church), this ship is on a secure journey towards salvation. It is the individual's choice whether he wants to be on this ship or not. If the individual does, he is part of the elect and his salvation is secure, but if he chooses to bail out, then he's no longer part of the elect and he's lost.

In Thessalonians God did not intend the church to be for his wrath but for salvation. If we look in I Corinthians 1:27-30.

27 God chose what is foolish in the world to shame the wise, God chose what is weak in the world to shame the strong, 28 God chose what is low and despised in the world, even things that are not, to bring to nothing things that are, 29 so that no human being might boast in the presence of God.

The evidences of election (today) are calling and justification, while the marks of reprobation are either a lack of knowledge of Jesus Christ or a lack of sanctification.

Step 5 - Calling

While on the road to Damascus, Paul encountered the risen and exalted Jesus that he had been railing against by seeking to kill all who claimed to be Christians! He was proud of how effective and efficient he was in this endeavor, but there came a time when he too would become effective and efficient as a Christian as he was in assassinating them.

Up until this point, Paul had heeded the claims of Gamaliel, expecting those who were following Jesus to eventually fall away (see Acts 5:34-39). Instead, Paul became a follower, becoming called an "apostle to the Gentiles" (Romans 11:13). Paul was soon to understand what Jesus meant when he said, "for I will show him how much he must suffer for the sake of my name," (Acts 9:16). Paul truly suffered, and learned to be content in all situations (Philippians 4:11-13). We too are called to this faith of God through Christ Jesus to become obedient as he too was obedient!

The gospel call is the call to obedience as well as faith. We were once chaotic and out of order, disobedient, deceived and bound by diverse lusts and wickedness. Full of jealousy and treachery not willing to love as God has loved us, forgive as we have been forgiven, but through his loving kindness and tender mercy we find our place of safety in the still small voice that is calling out to us!

Step 6 - Regeneration

Now we who have answered the calling are being retooled if you would. We are going through gene tranfusion and transplants from the old nature into the new and divine nature.

According to, II Peter 1:4 says "Whereby are given unto us exceeding great and precious promises: that by these ye might be partakers of the divine nature, having escaped the corruption that is in the world through lust." When regeneration begins in a new believers life it will continue until the day of his return!

When the goodness and loving kindness of God our Savior appeared, he saved us, not because of works done by us in righteousness, but according to his own mercy, by the washing of regeneration and renewal of the Holy Spirit, whom he poured out on us richly through Jesus Christ our Savior, so that being justified by his grace we might become heirs according to the hope of eternal life. Titus 3:3-7

Regeneration is the spiritual transformation in a person, brought about by the Holy Spirit, that brings the individual from being spiritually dead to become a spiritually alive human being. Regeneration is another way of speaking about the new birth or the second birth or being born again.

This subjective change worked in one's soul by the grace of God is variously designated in Scripture as a new birth, a resurrection, a new life, a new creature, a renewing of the mind, a dying to sin and living to righteousness, a translation from darkness to light.

Matthew 19:28, Jesus says to the twelve, "Truly, I say to you, in the new world when the Son of Man will sit on his glorious throne, you who have followed me will also sit on twelve thrones, judging the twelve tribes of Israel."

One's inherently sinful nature is profoundly and miraculously changed by regeneration—the new birth—so that person can respond to God in Faith, and live in accordance with His will (Matt. 19:28; John 3:3,5,7; Titus 3:5). No one can come alive to God apart from the Spirit's work.

Regeneration through the death, burial, resurrection and ascencion of Jesus Christ the whole of creation has gone through a reclamation, it has not yet become what it shall be when Jesus returns but it has been placed back into the state of which God gave men to have dominion over!

John Piper points out that the new birth is conceived by Jesus as something that will happen to all creation, not just human beings. He explains that this is because the whole of creation is defiled and disordered as result of the Fall (Romans 8:20-23). The whole universe will replace its futility and corruption and disease and degeneration and disasters with a whole new order—a new heaven and a new earth. Therefore, the new birth for an individual person may be seen as "the first installment of the final, universal regeneration of the universe."

Regarding why individuals need this regeneration, Piper points to the poignant description of the human heart in Titus 3:3 for an explanation: "We ourselves were once foolish, disobedient, led astray, slaves to various passions and pleasures, passing our days in malice and envy, hated by others and hating one another."

The use of the figure of new birth to describe this change emphasizes two facts about it.

The first is its decisiveness. The regenerate man has forever ceased to be the man he was; his old life is over and a new life has begun; he is a new creature in Christ, buried with him out of reach of condemnation and raised with him into a new life of righteousness (see Rom. 6:3-11; 2 Cor. 5:17; Col. 3:9-11).

The second fact emphasized is the monergism of regeneration. Infants do not induce, or cooperate in, their own procreation and birth; no more can those who are "dead in trespasses and sins" prompt the quickening operation of God's Spirit within them (see Eph. 2:1-10). Spiritual vivification is a free, and to man mysterious, exercise of divine power (John 3:8), not explicable in terms of the combination or cultivation of existing human resources (John 3:6), not caused or induced by any human efforts (John 1:12-13) or merits (Titus 3:3-7), and not, therefore, to be equated with, or attributed to, any of the experiences, decisions, and acts to which it gives rise and by which it may be known to have taken place.

At the end of Titus 3:5, Paul describes regeneration as a cleansing and a renewing by the Holy Spirit. The Spirit gives life (John 6:63). Jesus says, "I am the way the truth and the life" (John 14:6).

One may engage in all the outward duties of religion, and yet not be born again. They may advance to a great deal of strictness in their own way of religion, and yet be strangers to the new birth.

Regeneration is a real thorough change, whereby one is made a new creature (2 Cor. 5:17). The Lord God makes the creature a new creature, "as the goldsmith melts down the vessel of dishonor, and makes it a vessel of honor."

It is a change into the likeness of God. "We, beholding, as in a glass, the glory of the Lord, are changed into the same image" (2 Cor. 3:18).

Step 7 - Conversion

The Shaw Pocket Bible Handbook says that conversion is, "The decisive act in which a sinner turns away from sin in genuine repentance and accepts the salvation that Christ offers. The imagery in conversion is that of turning. A person is going along a road and realizes that he or she is on the wrong track. They will never reach the destination if they continue in that direction.

So the person "turns," or "is converted." He or she ceases to go in the wrong direction and begins going in the right one. Conversion changes the direction of one's course of life from the wrong way to the right way, the way that God wants." What does conversion involve for an individual? The Word of God, The Holy Spirit, and the Will of the individual. Jesus said that unless we are born again (or "born from above"), we will not see the kingdom of God (John 3:3).

Step 8 - Justification

Justification is the doctrine that God pardons, accepts, and declares a sinner to be "just" on the basis of Christ's righteousness (Rom 3:24-26; 4:25; 5:15-21) which results in God's peace (Rom 5:1), His Spirit (Rom 8:4), and salvation.

Justification is by grace through faith in Jesus Christ apart from all works and merit of the sinner (cf. Rom 1:18-3:28).

The Act of Justification

One-time act

Justification is a legal act, wherein God deems the sinner righteous on the basis of Christ's righteousness. Unlike Sanctification, Justification is not a process, but is a one-time act, complete and definitive.

The word justification is not always used in the same sense. Some even speak of a fourfold justification as a justification from eternity, a justification from the resurrection, a justification in final judgment – as these are all true.

Double Imputation

God's act of justification may be seen to involve a double imputation. On the one hand, the sin and guilt of the believer are imputed to Christ. On the other hand, the righteousness of Christ is imputed to the believer, whereby he is declared righteous.

Forgiveness and Adoption

Justification is seen in two parts: (1) The sinner is forgiven on the basis of Christ's righteousness. The pardon does not merely cover sins already committed – but reaches to all sins. (2) The sinner is adopted as a child of God. God places them within his household, giving them all the rights of heirs and children (Rom 8:17, 1 Peter 1:4).

The instrumental cause of justification: Faith

Justification is an act of God's free grace, wherein he pardoneth all our sins, and accepteth us as righteous in his sight, only for the righteousness of Christ imputed to us, and received by faith alone.

[With regard to faith and works, what matters] is whether the entailment is that of identity, cause, or inclusion. The first equates faith and works and destroys the whole Biblical teaching of justification by faith alone apart from the works of the law (Romans 3:28). The third subsumes works under faith and likewise destroys sola fide.

Only the second maintains the Biblical distinction between faith and works and the Biblical doctrine that works are the necessary consequence of faith and so upholds the Biblical teaching of justification by faith alone apart from the works of the law."

Step 9 - Adoption

"Adoption is that privilege, bestowed upon those who are united with Christ, and justified by faith, by which they are admitted into the family of God, adopted as his children, and made joint heirs with his own Son."

Although it has legal connotations, adoption is distinguished from justification.

It is also distinguished from regeneration. While regeneration refers to being spiritually reborn into the family of God, the concept of adoption refers to being included in a family one was not born into. It is essentially relational. Through adoption, we relate to God the Father as our Father-Savior, to Jesus as our brother and co-heir and fellow sufferer, and to the Spirit as our leader and pledge (or "down payment") of our inheritance in Christ.

Step 10 - Union with Christ

The theme of union with Christ occurs in numerous places in the New Testament, and is also pictured in the Old Testament.[1] It is that union enjoyed by believers, individually and corporately, with the Lord Jesus. It is sometimes referred to as the unio mystica or mystic union, as its fact is established without understanding the mechanism. Our union with Christ is best understood by the picture-language used in the Bible, and by the blessings we derive from our union with Christ.

The Language of Union with Christ

Jesus (in John's gospel), John and Paul all talked about union with Christ, each using different language to point to the one reality. There are also Old Testament and New Testament pictures of union which point forward to the antitype.

The most prevalent picture of union with Christ is that of being clothed in another. Adam and Eve, naked and ashamed in the Garden, are clothed with garments of skin (Gen. 3:21) and Jacob appears before his father in skins to appear as though his brother, Esau. Adam and Eve's shame is covered through the death of another, and Jacob only acquires blessing in his elder brother.

The Psalms also hint at union with God when they talk of finding the LORD to be a fortress and a refuge (e.g. Ps. 18:2), while the later Prophets frequently use the imagery of a husband and a wife to describe the relationship between God and Israel, an image picked up in the New Testament.

In John's gospel, Jesus describes himself as the Vine, and the disciples as branches in him (John 15:1–17). This is an extended metaphor, in which the Father is the gardener, and Jesus describes how unfruitful branches will be cut off, and that the only way to bear fruit is to remain in the vine. Branches which wither or are cut off are thrown in to the fire and burned, but the chosen branches will bear fruit which will last. Jesus goes on to say that his disciples do not belong to the world, but (by implication) they belong to him.

In his first epistle, John picks up much of that language, writing "Those who obey his commands live in him, and he in them. And this is how we know that he lives in us: We know it by the Spirit he gave us." Union with Christ means more than simply drawing one's life from Christ; it means living in him. Further, through our union with Christ, we enjoy union with the Father, since by seeing "that what you have heard from the beginning remains in you ... you also will remain in the Son and in the Father." (1 John 2:24)

In the Book of Revelation, John "heard what sounded like a great multitude ... shouting: 'Hallelujah! ... the wedding of the Lamb has come, and his bride has made herself ready. Fine linen, bright and clean, was given her to wear.' (Fine linen stands for the righteous acts of the saints.)" (Rev. 19:6–8) Once again, this picks up on previous language, but here it is the Old

Testament picture of being clothed with another which is brought through.

It is Paul's epistles that the fullest treatment of the theme of union with Christ is to be found. That union is the bedrock of the logic in Romans and the wellspring of praise in Ephesians. In Ephesians 2:20–21, Paul uses the picture of building the Church "on the foundation of the apostles and prophets, with Christ Jesus himself as the chief cornerstone. In him the whole building is joined together and rises to become a holy temple in the Lord." A similar picture can be found in 1 Corinthians 3:10–11, where this time, Paul describes Jesus himself as the foundation of the building, which seems to be the Church, described a few verses later as God's temple.

In Ephesians 5:30–32, Paul describes the relationship of Christ and the Church as being like that between a husband and wife. He also likens the Church to a body, of which Christ is the Head. This picture is developed in much more detail by Paul in 1 Corinthians 12:12–27, with particular respect to the importance of unity.

Another aspect of union with Christ is that of "Christ in us". Paul uses such language in Galatians, where he writes "I have been crucified with Christ and I no longer live, but Christ lives in me. The life I live in the body, I live by faith in the Son of God, who loved me and gave himself for me." (Gal. 2:20) In Chapter 1 of Colossians, Paul writes that "God has chosen to make known among the Gentiles the glorious riches of this mystery, which is Christ in you, the hope of glory."

The pictures taken as a whole, and considering other biblical language, allow us to see that there are two components to union with Christ: we in Christ, and Christ in us. It is a bond secured through faith (Gal. 3:20, Eph. 3:17) and sealed in baptism (Rom. 6:3–4, Gal. 3:26–27), and, as Ephesians 1:3–14 tells us, is a Trinitarian bond:

the Father is the source of our union;

the Son is the object of our union; and

the Spirit is the bond of our union. [1]

The Blessings of Union with Christ

The chief blessing of union with Christ is the blessing of the promises of God, for it is in Christ that all God's promises are "yea" and "amen", and when found in him, we become partakers of those promises (Eph. 3:6). We may well say, then, that it is on account of Christ that we enjoy all the good things God so richly bestows.

We shall divide the blessings under three heads: blessings for believers with respect to God, with respect to one another and with respect to themselves.

Blessings to Believers Towards God

Grudem does well to observe that ... every aspect of God's relationship to believers is in some way connected to our relationship with Christ. From God's counsels in eternity past before the world was created, to our fellowship with God in heaven in eternity future, and including every aspect of our relationship with God in this life—all has occurred in union with Christ.

Paul begins his meditation on union with Christ in Ephesians 1 with a shout of "praise be to the God and Father of our Lord Jesus Christ, who has blessed us in the heavenly realms with every spiritual blessing in Christ!" In what follows, he explicitly grounds election, adoption, grace and redemption "in Christ", culminating in the first peak, looking towards the time when God will "bring all things in heaven and on earth together under one head, even Christ."

He then begins again with election in Christ, reminding the Ephesians that they, too, "were included in Christ when [they] heard the word of truth, the gospel of [their] salvation."

In Romans 6–7, Paul expounds union with Christ with respect to sin and the Law, showing us that we are dead to sin but alive to God in Christ Jesus. His argument is that, since we died (in Christ) to the Law, we died also to sin (since where there is no Law, there is no sin), and are now under grace. We have also been raised to new life in Christ's resurrection, and will, one day, be renewed in our bodies, in the power of Christ's resurrection. This is part of the hope of glory mentioned by Paul in his letter to the Colossians. Imputation, of our sin to Christ, and his righteousness to us, also occur in union with Christ: hiding in him, the punishment for our sin falls on him; clothed in him, the righteousness of his life becomes our own.

Blessings to Believers Towards Others

The main theme of union with Christ as it affects our relationships is to promote unity in the Church: being united vertically with Christ, we are naturally united horizontally with each other. In 1 Corinthians 12, Paul describes the different talents and gifts as being analogous to different parts of the body: eyes, hands, feet etc. Therefore, we should seek to build each other up in our respective gifts.

In Galatians 3:28, Paul's argument is that, since all are one in Christ Jesus, there is then "neither Jew nor Gentile, slave nor free, male nor female"— there is no place for discrimination on the basis of the status into which someone was born, as all are born again into the same status in Christ.

Blessings to Believers Towards Self

When found in the Vine, branches enjoy growth and produce fruit. Believers can be assured that, on the basis of their union with Christ, they will experience a long-term pattern of growth, as Christ in them conforms them to his likeness. Discipline is another of the blessings of union with Christ, as we are pruned by the Father so as to bear fruit. We also enjoy protection when found in Christ, who makes himself our shield and stronghold. Paul's wonderful description of the armour of God is truly the armour of Christ, as each piece he describes is to be found only in union with Jesus, who alone is truth and righteousness.

Finally, "our hearts are restless, until they find their rest in thee" (attrib. St. Augustine). It is only in Christ that we find our true identity, for he is the true Man.

Step 11 - Sanctification

Sanctification, or in its verbal form, sanctify, literally means "to set apart" for special use or purpose, that is, to make holy or sacred. Therefore, sanctification refers to the state or process of being set apart, i.e. made holy. In systematic theology, the term often carries a technical meaning that differs from the biblical word group. Sanctification is regularly equated with the Christian life. In Christianity, the term can be used to refer to objects which are set apart for special purposes, but the most common use within Christian theology is in reference to the change brought about by God in a believer, begun at the point of salvation or justification and continuing throughout the life of the believer. Many forms of Christianity believe that this process will only be completed in Heaven when believers are also glorified, but some believe that complete holiness is possible in life.

Progressive Sanctification

"Indeed, the more sanctified the person is, the more conformed he is to the image of his Savior, the more he must recoil against every lack of conformity to the holiness of God. The deeper his apprehension of the majesty of God, the greater the intensity of his love to God, the more persistent his yearning for the attainment of the prize of the high calling of God in Christ Jesus, the more conscious will he be of the gravity of the sin that remains and the more poignant will be his detestation of it....Was this not the effect in all the people of God as they came into closer proximity to the revelation of God's holiness." –

John Murray,

Redemption Accomplished and Applied

Definitive Sanctification

This is a section stub. Please edit it to add information.

Reference Scriptures:

- Leviticus 11:44 - "…Consecrate yourselves therefore, and be holy, for I am holy. …"

- Matthew 5:48 - "You therefore must be perfect, as your heavenly Father is perfect."

- Romans 6:22 - "But now that you have been set free from sin and have become slaves of God, the fruit you get leads to sanctification and its end, eternal life."

- I Corinthians 6:11 - "…But you were washed, you were sanctified, you were justified in the name of the Lord Jesus Christ and by the Spirit of our God."

- II Corinthians 3:18 - "And we all, with unveiled face, beholding the glory of the Lord, are being transformed into the same image from one degree of glory to another. For this comes from the Lord who is the Spirit."

- II Corinthians 7:1 - "...beloved, let us cleanse ourselves from every defilement of body and spirit, bringing holiness to completion in the fear of God."

- I Thesssalonians 4:3 - "For this is the will of God, your sanctification..."

- I Thesssalonians 4:7 - "For God has not called us for impurity, but in holiness."

- I Thesssalonians 5:23 - "Now may the God of peace himself sanctify you completely, and may your whole spirit and soul and body be kept blameless at the coming of our Lord Jesus Christ."

- Hebrews 6:1 - "Therefore let us leave the elementary doctrine of Christ and go on to maturity…"

- Hebrews 12:14 - "Strive for peace with everyone, and for the holiness without which no one will see the Lord."

- James 1:4 - "And let steadfastness have its full effect, that you may be perfect and complete, lacking in nothing."

- I Peter 1:15-16 - "…but as he who called you is holy, you also be holy in all your conduct, since it is written, 'You shall be holy, for I am holy…'"

- I John 4:18 - "There is no fear in love, but perfect love casts out fear. For fear has to do with punishment, and whoever fears has not been perfected in love."

Through Sanctification – Jehovah M'Kaddesh

(Marilyn Hickey, excerpted from the Names of God, pp. 98,106,109,110)

"Have you ever had a strong desire to have your personality to line up perfectly with the Lord's personality? Jesus wants you to have a total image of Himself living through you. He gives you that image in the name Jehovah M'Kaddesh ...first found in Leviticus 20:7,8... many Christians drift here and wander there --not really knowing God's plan for them.

They know about the possibility of having a deeper relationship with Him, and they know about the baptism of the Holy Spirit, and some even may be baptized in the Holy Spirit, but there seems to be no growth, nor a real hunger for growth...It is because there is something lacking, and the key is in the name Jehovah

M'Kaddesh…it is the way in which the revealing One would have his people walk… to **sanctify means to consecrate, to dedicate, or to become holy…**being set apart…to walk in total dedication to Him…everything the Jewish people did in the Bible, and today all relate back to their God…God did not do all of the sanctifying…within the name Jehovah M'Kaddesh will not allow us to believe a lie, but tell us the truth that men must choose holiness ….Nebuchadnezzar's spirit came in line with the Lord. What happened? His mind, intellect, reasoning, and physical body changed from being like an animal's. He became a man of God…I Thes. 4:3,…talks about keeping your entire spirit, soul, and body blameless…God doesn't want you to have little hidden closets and missed motivations.

How do you sanctify yourself? …relying totally on Him in Everything!

Jehovah M'Kaddesh appears over 700 times...because God wants a people who are set apart unto Him...When you belong to God, you have been set apart...not in flesh...mind...alone won't cut it...you must be set apart to serve Him in spirit and in truth!

God called Jonah to prophesy to Nineveh...Jonah had a problem...he had mixed motivations...He wanted to obey God's call only when it suited him. Although he loved God with all of his mind, his spirit was not set apart...Jonah had some time to think things over, inside of the grave within a seemingly bottomless pit (fish). He totally consecrated himself, spirit and all, unto the Lord God (this is a prophecy in symbolism, that foretold the death, burial, and time in hell to accomplish the resurrection of us all, through Christ Jesus).

Unlike Jonah, who even after he obeyed, returned to the way he was before… Because his spirit had not been sanctified….for I the Lord your God am holy…the word "holiness" confuses many people, but…think of it this way: when you set yourself apart unto God, you will be whole - you will be holy… He just wants us complete, starting with our spirits…when it is in right relationship with God, your soul and body will line up…your soul and body are just things that your spirit wears.

Holiness, is a setting apart, that begins with the wholeness of God inside of you. Every 7th year is the Year of Jubilee, after the children of Israel had observed the solemn fasting and feasting; after having set apart themselves, and everything they had in their possessions for 7 Sabbath moons. (Which were times of honoring the Lord for his continual care).

The 7th year was ushered in, redemption proclaimed, and liberty for all who were in bondage, is celebrated the entire year. Is this the seventh year approaching US and perhaps passed as you are reading this book.

ARE YOU READY!!! If not GET OUT OF MY WAY!!! I AM COMING THROUGH!!!

What hinders you that you can not run? (read Galatians 5:7)

And be ready, to celebrate the Year of Jubilee, symbolically this can be yours everyday, we do not have to wait for the annual fasting and feasting. Because a more excellent way has been prepared through Christ Jesus, so that you may have Jubilee every day, moment, and second of your life.

MAY BLESSING, AND HONOR BE HIS!!!

Step 12 - Perseverance

The doctrine of perseverance is rooted in God's unconditional election and predestination. That is, since God is the One who chose and predestined the elect to salvation, therefore the elect will be saved. They might turn away from faith and give appearance of losing their salvation, but if they really are elect they will repent and ultimately return to faith, because God is the One ensuring their salvation. This doctrine is also closely related to the doctrine of justification and adoption. Because God is the One who justifies the elect, no one can bring any condemnation on them. In the same way because those who truly believe in Christ are adopted as God's sons, they cannot be condemned to eternal punishment.

Eternal Security

"Eternal security" is often seen as synonymous with "Perseverance of the saints." That is, a person who truly trusts in Christ, may have assurance of eternal life with God, and thus be eternally secure. Historically, this comes from a biblical, Calvinistic framework, wherein salvation is secure because the perseverance of the saved person is certain. Today, however, the doctrine of eternal security is usually expressed without the reference to the perseverance (or continuance) and other means of grace indicative of true saving/justifying faith. This mind-set goes hand-in-hand with the "easy believism" and "carnal Christianity" so prevalent in the evangelical church today. It is characterized by the trite phrase "once saved, always saved", suggesting that one may continue in a life of willful sin and be confident of salvation because he has made a profession of faith in the past. This goes against biblical exhortations, warnings for final salvation and qualifications of true saving faith.

For example :

John 15:6 "If anyone does not abide in Me, he is thrown away as a branch and dries up; and they gather them, and cast them into the fire and they are burned."

Heb 12:14 "Pursue peace with all men, and the sanctification without which no one will see the Lord."

Eph 5:5-6 "For this you know with certainty, that no immoral or impure person or covetous man, who is an idolater, has an inheritance in the kingdom of Christ and God. Let no one deceive you with empty words, for because of these things the wrath of God comes upon the sons of disobedience."

I John 2:3-4 "By this we know that we have come to know Him, if we keep His commandments. The one who says, "I have come to know Him," and does not keep His commandments, is a liar, and the truth is not in him;"

I Cor. 10:1-6 "For I do not want you to be unaware, brethren, that our fathers were all under the cloud and all passed through the sea; and all were baptized into Moses in the cloud and in the sea; and all ate the same spiritual food; and all drank the same spiritual drink, for they were drinking from a spiritual rock which followed them; and the rock was Christ. Nevertheless, with most of them God was not well-pleased; for they were laid low in the wilderness."

II Cor 13:5 "Test yourselves {to see} if you are in the faith; examine yourselves! Or do you not recognize this about yourselves, that Jesus Christ is in you--unless indeed you fail the test?"

James 2:14-17 "What use is it, my brethren, if someone says he has faith but he has no works?

Can that faith save him? If a brother or sister is without clothing and in need of daily food, and one of you says to them, "Go in peace, be warmed and be filled," and yet you do not give them what is necessary for their body, what use is that? Even so faith, if it has no works, is dead, being by itself."

Definitive wandering is deadly and maybe a sign that one is not truly saved. Christians in the bible are warned and encouraged over and over again to not give up, but to persevere in faith in order to be saved. "Blessed is the man who remains steadfast under trial," as James says, "for when he has stood the test he will receive the crown of life, which God has promised to those who love him." (James 1:12)

Romans 8:29 "For those whom He foreknew, He also predestined to become conformed to the image of His Son, so that He would be the firstborn among many brethren"

Jeremiah 32:40 "I will make an everlasting covenant with them that I will not turn away from them, to do them good; and I will put the fear of Me in their hearts so that they will not turn away from Me."

Romans 14:4 "Who are you to judge the servant of another? To his own master he stands or falls; and he will stand, for the Lord is able to make him stand."

Philippians 1:6: "And I am sure of this, that he who began a good work in you will bring it to completion at the day of Jesus Christ."

Jude 1:24 "Now to Him who is able to keep you from stumbling, and to make you stand in the presence of His glory blameless with great joy"

I Peter 1:3-5 "Blessed be the God and Father of our Lord Jesus Christ, who according to His great mercy has caused us to be born again to a living hope through the resurrection of Jesus Christ from the dead, to obtain an inheritance which is imperishable and undefiled and will not fade away, reserved in heaven for you, who are protected by the power of God through faith for a salvation ready to be revealed in the last time"

John 10:28-29: "I give them eternal life, and they will never perish, and no one will snatch them out of my hand. My Father, who has given them to me, is greater than all, and no one is able to snatch them out of the Father's hand."

Romans 11:29: "For the gifts and the calling of God are irrevocable."

I Corinthians 15:1-2 - "Now I would remind you, brothers, of the gospel I preached to you, which you received, in which you stand, and by which you are being saved, if you hold fast to the word I preached to you—unless you believed in vain."

Hebrews 3:14 - "For we have become partakers of Christ, if we hold fast the beginning of our assurance firm until the end"

Hebrews 3:6 - "but Christ was faithful as a Son over His house—whose house we are, if we hold fast our confidence and the boast of our hope firm until the end."

Col 1:22-23 "yet He has now reconciled you in His fleshly body through death, in order to present you before Him holy and blameless and beyond reproach— if indeed you continue in the faith firmly established and steadfast, and not moved away from the hope of the gospel that you have heard, which was proclaimed in all creation under heaven, and of which I, Paul, was made a minister."

Matthew 24:12-13 "Because lawlessness is increased, most people's love will grow cold. But the one who endures to the end, he will be saved" (cf. Mark 13:13)

Matthew 10:22 "You will be hated by all because of My name, but it is the one who has endured to the end who will be saved."

Galatians 6:9 - "And let us not grow weary of doing good, for in due season we will reap, if we do not give up."

James 5:19-20 - "My brothers, if anyone among you wanders from the truth and someone brings him back, let him know that whoever brings back a sinner from his wandering will save his soul from death and will cover a multitude of sins."

Phil 2:12-13 "So then, my beloved, just as you have always obeyed, not as in my presence only, but now much more in my absence, work out your salvation with fear and trembling; for it is

God who is at work in you, both to will and to work for His good pleasure."

Acts 4:27-29 "For truly in this city there were gathered together against Your holy servant Jesus, whom You anointed, both Herod and Pontius Pilate, along with the Gentiles and the peoples of Israel, to do whatever Your hand and Your purpose predestined to occur.

And now, Lord, take note of their threats, and grant that Your bond-servants may speak Your word with all confidence".

II Tim 2:24-25 "The Lord's bond-servant must not be quarrelsome, but be kind to all, able to teach, patient when wronged, with gentleness correcting those who are in opposition, if perhaps God may grant them repentance leading to the knowledge of the truth"

II Sam 17:14 "Then Absalom and all the men of Israel said, "The counsel of Hushai the Archite is better than the counsel of Ahithophel." For the LORD had ordained to thwart the good counsel of Ahithophel, so that the LORD might bring calamity on Absalom."

I Sam 2:23-25 "He said to them, "Why do you do such things, the evil things that I hear from all these people? "No, my sons; for the report is not good which I hear the LORD'S people circulating.

"If one man sins against another, God will mediate for him; but if a man sins against the LORD, who can intercede for him?" But they would not listen to the voice of their father, for the LORD desired to put them to death."

Step 13 - Glorification

John 17:20 "And those He predestined, He also called; those He called, He also justified; those He justified, He also glorified" (Romans 8:30).

Glorification is the third step in the justification-sanctification-glorification chain. Glorification has not yet occurred; it occurs at Christ's return. Paul describes it this way: "For the trumpet will sound, the dead will be raised imperishable, and we will be changed. For the perishable must clothe itself with the imperishable, and the mortal with immortality" (I Corinthians 15:52-53).

Our own physical bodies will experience glorification. We will not be changed into some sort of spirit-entity as many of the cults teach. Jesus Himself demonstrated this when He appeared to the disciples after the resurrection:

"Though the doors were locked, Jesus came and stood among them and said, 'Peace be with you!' Then He said to Thomas, 'Put your finger here; see My hands. Reach out your hand and put it into My side. Stop doubting and believe'" (John 20:26-27). Luke 24:29 also affirms that the glorified body is not a mere spirit-body; if it were,

Christ would be a deceiver since He claimed that it was His own body: "They were startled and frightened, thinking they saw a ghost. He said to them, 'Why are you troubled, and why do doubts rise in your minds? Look at My hand and My feet. It is I Myself! Touch me and see; a ghost does not have flesh and bones, as you see I have.'"

It is at the time of glorification that the sanctification process is fully complete -- our bodies will be changed, the old sin nature will be eliminated, and we will see the risen Christ in all his glory: "Now we see but a poor reflection as in a mirror; then we shall see face to face. Now I know in part; then I shall know fully, even as I am fully known" (I Corinthians 13:12).

"Meanwhile we groan, longing to be clothed with our heavenly dwelling, because when we are clothed, we will not be found naked. For while we are in this tent, we groan and are burdened, because we do not wish to be unclothed but to be clothed with our heavenly dwelling, so that what is mortal may be swallowed up by life" (II Corinthians 5:2-4).

Step 14 – Salvation

Must now be worked out with fear and trembling not by works! Working it out is allowing the 13 Steps of the process perfect us in the completion of running the race of the 14th Step "SALVATION". We must go through our own transfiguration our Mount Tabor moment lies ahead and not behind! We must allow the Holy Spirit to do in us what the Father wills through his divine purpose and plan for our lives. What more can we add to this? Nothing!

It is FINISHED! Jesus spoke those words out of his own mouth! And Jesus said he would not speak except what the Father gave him to speak! We must now come to see that the price for us has been paid! When you buy something for your personal usage you have full expectations for it to work according to what the manufacturer has advertised and what your own perceptions are of what it should do to enhance your life! When God purchased our salvation through Jesus Christ should he not have expectations from us? In listening to a Messianic Pastor speak about how irreverent we are in the earth; he shared a Jewish Proverb that I will paraphrase here. "If God lived on earth in a house we would break out his windows" Selah! When we have blamed God, been angry at God or angry at his leaders, we would have vandalized Gods' house, egged it, toilet papered it and worst! Could it be this is what we do in the church house, we break out – disrespect the holiness of the place we have erected to worship because we have no reverence for God! How often would you allow someone to come to your home and disrespect it and your possessions! God has feelings!

Chapter 7
The Mount Of Transfiguration

7- The Mount of Transfiguration

We see this mountain "Mount Tabor" recorded in the 17th Chapter of St. Matthew's Gospel, and it is called the Mount of Transfiguration. On this mountain we have a wonderfully interesting piece of history. The disciples had been with Jesus almost three years and had only seen Him as a man. But on the mount they saw Him in His glorified body. We read that His face did shine as the sun and His raiment was as white as the light. Then we read, "And behold there appeared unto them Moses and Elias talking with him;" and we turn back and notice that it had been 1451 years since Moses had his funeral on the mountain top across the River Jordan from the promised land. After the death of Moses we hear nothing more of him for 1451 years, but to our surprise here he is on the Mt of Transfiguration. We look at the other fellow who is on the mount and behold it is

Elijah, and this is around 896 years later.

So we have before us the Law-giver and the prophet and the Savior. The Savior had said that he would not pass away until all the Law and the Prophets were fulfilled, and now here on this mountain we have in the presence of three witnesses, Peter, James and John, the Christ of the Old and New Testaments. Now here stands before us the man that gave the Law to the world, and we have before us the greatest Prophet that ever lived. No other man ever did such things as Elijah.

The prayer that brought the three years' famine and the prayer that brought the rain, and the prayer that brought the fire from heaven, and the slaying of eight hundred and fifty false prophets.

When we read that Peter wanted to build three houses and live on the mountain top we are not surprised, for today if we were to get into the presence of the Son of God, and if Moses and Elias were to appear on the scene, we would want to stay there and ask questions about our loved ones.

In this wonderful scene on the mountain top we have three great proofs before us, and they are as follows: We have Moses there to represent all the dead, and he proves the resurrection. In the case of Moses we see that the dead will be resurrected and will stand at the Judgment Bar of God as natural as if they had never died. We see this proven by Moses, for here is a man that had been dead 1451 years, and we see him as natural as if he had never died. So Moses on the Mount

of Transfiguration represents all the dead in Christ. We remember that Elijah never died but was translated, and went up without ever tasting death, but there he stands on the mountain top as natural as if he had just come from Mt. Carmel. In this wonderful transfiguration we see that Elijah represents all the living, for he never died. He never became an angel while he was gone. He still remained the old Prophet, and the moment that Peter flashed his eyes on him he knew him and called him by name. So that proves that we will know each other in the Land so fair. Some people have always had their doubts as to whether we will know each other in heaven or not. Well, we need have no more trouble about that. We surely will have as much sense in heaven as we have on earth. We know our loved ones here and of course we will know them there. Another fact that we have brought out on the Mount of Transfiguration is that we have settled forever who is to be our leader. While the face of the Lord was shining like the sun, we hear the voice of the Father saying, "This is my well beloved Son, hear him."

Notice He did not say to hear Moses, or to hear Elijah, but He said "hear him," that is, hear

Christ. While we are to honor all men to whom honor is due, we are to hear the Son of God and we are to obey Him and Him only. The preacher of the gospel is to hear the Son of God and get his messages from Him, and they are to be fresh from heaven; not man-made, but heaven-born; not to be reasoned out, but they are to be revealed from heaven to the God-made preacher and not the schoolmade man.

Schools may help a man a little, but if a man only has what schools can give him he is to be pitied, for the poorest preachers on earth are men who are just out of school full of self and ignorant of God, and as empty as a tin horn, with no knowledge of God or of the blessed Holy Ghost. I am sure the Lord would use a man with good education if He could get him, but the trouble is this: when a man goes a few years to the schools and finds out enough to make him useful, the devil jumps on the poor fellow with both feet and stamps him into the ground, and makes him believe that he is too important to give his useful life to the Church of the Lord Jesus, and the thing for him to do is to go into the things of the world: Law or Medicine, or the stage. Most anything will beat being a preacher.

And so the devil catches the most of the men out of the schools, but the Lord in His divine providence just takes boys and girls out of the corn fields or from the cook stove or the wash tub and converts them and then sanctifies them and fills them with the Holy Ghost and puts them out on exhibition for the world to look at.

He gives them mounts of transfiguration and reveals Himself to them, and the Scriptures all open up to such a fellow and he lives in and revels in the Holy Bible.

He has mounts of holy worship, and mountains of law, and mountains of vision and mountains of possession, then mountains of contest, and mountains of temptation, and mountains of blessing, and then his mount of choice, and at last his mount of trans-figuration, where he will know Moses as the lawgiver, and Elijah as the great prophet, and, thank God! He will know the Son of God as his Leader, and his Guide, and his Protector, and his Keeper, and his all and in all.

He will be a living, walking example of what God can do for a man in this old world, and he will live the mountain-top life which is nothing more or less than the blessing of holiness as a second work of grace, received by faith subsequent to regeneration. The mountain-top life is the one, and don't you stop short of it, beloved; don't you listen to the devil any longer, but press your claim to the throne of grace and tell your heavenly Father that you have come after a mountain, and that you will not be satisfied with a mole hill, or a big ridge; nothing short of a mountain will satisfy you in this world. Well, glory to God! Amen!

Changing the Guard

(Lordship)

Is and has God, through his Son Jesus Christ the Anointed One and His Anointing become Lord and Savior of your life? How do you discern when this has happened? Well, as Paul said, it is no longer I but, Christ that lives in me (Gal. 2:20). But the comforter, which is the Holy Spirit, whom the father will send in my name, he shall teach you all things, and bring all things to your remembrance, whatsoever I have said unto you. He empowers us when the Holy Spirit is come upon us, and we become witnesses unto him both in Jerusalem, and in all Judaea, and in Samaria, and unto the uttermost part of the earth. (Acts 1:8)

We are no longer led away by every wind and doctrine, but He has become the light unto our feet and pathway. "Howbeit when he the Holy Spirit of Truth, is come, he will guide you into all truth, for he shall not speak of himself, but whatsoever he shall hear, that shall he speak, and he will show you things to come." (John 16:13)

"He is in control, and, "While Peter thought on the vision, the Spirit said unto him, Behold, three men seek thee. Arise therefore, and get thee down, and go with them, doubting nothing: for I have sent them." (Acts 10:19-20)

When someone is in control of a situation or person, the exact thing that is desired, by the controlling person is what is usually accomplished if they have absolute or enough power over that individual or thing. Which means that when we allow God, He is and can be the operator of our souls.

"Now when they had gone throughout Phrygia and the region of Galatia, and were forbidden of the Holy Ghost (Spirit) to preach the word in Asia, After they were come to Mysia. They assayed to go into Bithynia: but the Spirit suffered them not."(Acts 16:6-7)

We receive the constrainment of God when we are in continual fellowship with the Father is interrupted when we choose to follow our natural mind, and our non-divine nature. For as many as are led by the Spirit of God, they are the Sons of God. (Romans 8:14) We are reproved that we might not be lost with the world but receive eternal life. It is through obedience to Christ, that we are endowed with the life giving properties of salvation. "For the bread of God is he which cometh down from heaven, and giveth life unto the world." (John 6:33) We see God seated on the throne of one who is one-hearted and surrended to his Lordship!

Then when we no longer want to be in charge...

He becomes our Guide

"Howbeit when he, the Spirit of Truth, is come he will guide you into all truth; for he shall not speak of himself; but whatsoever he shall hear, that shall he speak; and he will show you things to come." (John 16:13)

He becomes our Controller

"While Peter thought on the vision, the spirit said unto him, behold, three men seek thee. Arise, therefore, and get thee down, and go with them, doubting nothing: for I have sent them." (Acts 10:19-20)

He becomes our Operator

"Now when they had gone throughout Phrygia and the region of Galatia, and were forbidden of the Holy Spirit to preach the word in Asia, after they were come to Mysia, they assayed to go into Bithynia: but the spirit suffered them not." (Acts

16:6)

He becomes our Reprover

"For as many as are led by the Spirit of God, they are the sons of God." (Romans 8:14)

He becomes our Life Giver

"For the bread of God is He which cometh down from Heaven, and giveth life unto the world." (John 6:33)

He becomes our Truth

"If ye had known me, ye should have known my father also: and from henceforth ye know him, and have seen him." (John 14:17)

He becomes our Comforter

"And I will pray the Father, and he shall give you another Comforter, that he may abide with you forever."(John 14:16)

He becomes our Teacher

"For the Holy Spirit shall teach you in the same hour what ye ought to say." (Luke 12:12)

And...

Our desires turn towards God, because our heart is no longer divided, into the past, present, future of what if or when. When the scripture speaks to us and says, now after having done all to stand, stand. (Eph. 6:13-14) As you know a house divided against itself cannot stand. Now submit our wills to God through the covenant according to Matthew 12:25-26.

Chapter 8

Original Sin

8- Original Sin

J.C. Ryle says, A proper understanding of the doctrine of original sin is essential for understanding justification and sanctification. A misunderstanding of original sin is likely to cause grave errors in the beliefs of an individual regarding these two vital areas. As August Pieper once said, "Any error taken to its logical conclusion will destroy faith." Thank God errors aren't always taken to their logical conclusion.

The sin of Adam and Eve held dire consequences, not only for them personally, but also for the rest of the human race. The guilt of their first transgression and the corruption of their nature is charged to all their children, including us who are alive today. This hereditary guilt and depravity is called original sin. Before the fall, man was created in the image of God (Gen 1:27). This perfect image of God consists of a perfect knowledge of God's will. Paul attests to this when he tells the Christians at Colosse that when they were brought to faith they "have put on the new self, which is being renewed in knowledge in the image of the Creator" (Col 3:10). Man was also created perfectly righteous and holy. The writer of Ecclesiastes said, "God made mankind upright" (Ec 8:12). Man was also created free of evil or sin. He was innocent. This can be seen in the fact that before the fall both Adam and Eve were naked but they felt no shame (Gen 2:25).

Man was created with a free will. The fact that he was able to sin is evident by the fact that he did sin. However, he also had the ability not to sin. "God saw all that he had made and it was very good" (Gen 1:31). Man was part of God's creation. He was declared "very good." This would imply he had the ability to be good.

The act of being good would mean that man had the ability not to sin.

How, could God declare something good if the ability not to sin were not present?

The picture changes drastically after the fall. Man lost the image of God because of the fall into sin.

Sin caused man to no longer be perfectly righteous and live a truly holy life. The innocence which was present before the fall is now gone. After the fall Adam and Eve realized they were naked and felt ashamed (Gen 3:8).

Because of the fall into sin man no longer possessed a free will. No longer was man able not to sin. After the fall, all men born in the natural way were born in the image and likeness of man (Gen 5:3). The image of man is sinful. Moses tells us that God looked down at man and saw that "the thoughts of his heart was only evil all the time" (Gen 6:5). From birth, man is steeped in sin. The Psalmist, David, wrote, "Surely I was sinful from birth, from the time my mother conceived me" (Ps 51:5). God tells us through the apostle Paul, "The wages of sin is death" (Ro 6:23). Babies die every day. It therefore must follow that babies are sinful. Man can no longer choose to love God or have faith in God. "The man without the Spirit does not accept the things that come from the Spirit of God, for they are foolishness to him, and he cannot understand them, because they are spiritually discerned" (I Cor 2:14). Man cannot keep God's commandments. Jesus proved this to the rich young ruler who came to him asking what must be done to inherit eternal life. The Greek word "archon" used in verse 28 of the eighteenth chapter, of the Gospel of Luke to identify the person means ruler. Used in this context, it refers to a ruler of one the local synagogues or councils.

These men were regarded as people who lived righteous lives. However, when the rich young ruler asked Jesus the question, Jesus replied,

"You know the commandments; Do not commit adultery, do not murder, do not steal, do not give false testimony, honor your father and your mother" (Lu 18:20). Jesus was recalling to the young man's memory the Decalogue. Anyone who measures themselves up against the commandments should quickly realize how miserably they have failed if they are honest with themselves and examine themselves as God examines men.

The point did not sink in for the rich ruler. He replied "All these I have kept since I was a boy" (Lu 18:21). Jesus had to prove to him that he had not kept all the commandments perfectly. He did this by challenging him. "You still lack one thing. Sell everything you have and give to the poor, and you will have treasure in heaven. Then come, follow me" (Lu 18:22). In saying this, Jesus proved that the man loved the things of this world more than he did heavenly things. This violates the first commandment. As the rich young ruler went away sad, the disciples were amazed. Knowing this man's reputation, they thought to themselves, if he cannot fulfill God's demands then who could? Who possibly could be saved? Jesus answered this question for them. He said "what is impossible with man is possible with God" (Lu 18:27). For man, keeping God's Law is impossible. Trusting in God, loving God, fearing God perfectly is an impossible task for man.

If one properly understands the doctrine of original sin, they are forced to look outside of themselves in their search for a way to be justified before God. However, the question that must be asked if salvation cannot be found in man where should man look?

Since all men are sinful, looking to another man or to human reason becomes foolishness. Salvation cannot be found there.

Since all other world religions teach that man must depend on his own good works to appease his God, the person understanding original sin will likewise be forced to rule out these religions. The Bible is the verbally inspired Word of God. Paul told his young protégé Timothy, "from infancy you have known the Holy Scriptures, which are able to make you wise for salvation" (II Tim 3:15). God's plan of salvation is outlined only in these pages. This is the only place we can find it.

I now propose to consider, in the last place, the distinction between justification and sanctification. Wherein do they agree, and wherein do they differ?

This branch of our subject is one of great importance, though I fear it will not seem so to all my readers. I shall handle it briefly, but I dare not pass it over altogether. Too many are apt to look at nothing but the surface of things in religion, and regard nice distinctions in theology as questions of" words and names," which are of little real value. But I warn all who are in earnest about their souls, that the discomfort which arises from not" distinguishing things that differ" in Christian doctrine is very great indeed;and I especially advise them, if they love peace, to seek clear views about the matter before us. Justification and sanctification are two distinct things we must always remember. Yet there are points in which they agree and points in which they differ. Let us try to find out what they are.

In what, then, are justification and sanctification alike?

(a) Both proceed originally from the free grace of God. It is of His gift alone that believers are justified or sanctified at all.

(b) Both are part of that great work of salvation which Christ, in the eternal covenant, has undertaken on behalf of His people. Christ is the fountain of life, from which pardon and holiness both flow. The root of each is Christ.

(c) Both are to be found in the same persons. Those who are justified are always sanctified, and those who are sanctified are always justified. God has joined them together, and they cannot be put asunder.

(d) Both begin at the same time. The moment a person begins to be a justified person; he also begins to be a sanctified person. He may not feel it, but it is a fact.

(e) Both are alike necessary to salvation. No one ever reached heaven without a renewed heart as well as forgiveness, without the Spirit's grace as well as the blood of Christ, without a meetness for eternal glory as well as a title. The one is just as necessary as the other.

Such are the points on which justification and sanctification agree.

Let us now reverse the picture, and see wherein they differ.

(a) Justification is the reckoning and counting a man to be righteous for the sake of another, even Jesus Christ the Lord. Sanctification is the actual making a man inwardly righteous, though it may be in a very feeble degree.

(b) The righteousness we have by our justification is not our own, but the everlasting perfect righteousness of our great Mediator Christ, imputed to us, and made our own by faith. The righteousness we have by sanctification is our own righteousness, imparted, inherent, and wrought in us by the Holy Spirit, but mingled with much infirmity and imperfection.

(c) In justification our own works have no place at all, and simple faith in Christ is the one thing needful.

(d) In sanctification our own works are of vast importance and God bids us fight, and watch, and pray, and strive, and take pains, and labour Justification is a finished and complete work, and a man is perfectly justified the moment he believes. Sanctification is an imperfect work, comparatively, and will never be perfected until we reach heaven.

(e) Justification admits of no growth or increase: a man is as much justified the hour he first comes to Christ by faith as he will be to all eternity. Sanctification is eminently a progressive work, and admits of continual growth and enlargement so long as a man lives.

(f) Justification has special reference to our persons, our standing in God's sight, and our deliverance from guilt. Sanctification has special reference to our natures, and the moral renewal of our hearts.

(g) Justification gives us our title to heaven, and boldness to enter in. Sanctification gives us our meetness for heaven, and prepares us to enjoy it when we dwell there.

(h) Justification is the act of God about us, and is not easily discerned by others. Sanctification is the work of God within us, and cannot be hid in its outward manifestation from the eyes of men.

Components of Salvation One(ness)

Redemption:

We have deliverance from the power of sin, the debt and the full acquittal of the guilt.

Blessings:

Instead of the curse of the Law of Sin which was death.

The parable of the grain of wheat is a symbolism of division and unity. Unless the seed falls into the ground and dies it remains alone. A grain of wheat's husk represents the outward life, the wrapping of the flesh) and the seed inside of the grain represents the life of the seed.

Until it is planted it remains alone, but once it falls into the soil and becomes one with the earth around it, and totally dependent on the nutrients of the soil to propel it to its purpose in life it is divided -- separated from its' purpose.

John 12:24 "Verily, verily, I say unto you, Except a corn of wheat fall into the ground and die, it abideth alone; but if it die, it bringeth forth much fruit."

The life of the spirit of Christ Jesus is the seed that is planted into the soil of our hearts. Unless that seed is allowed to die in us and go through the transformation of the crucifying of the flesh, the life of that seed will not be realized in the power of the resurrection will bring forth much fruit.

Our hearts are wholly dark without salvation. Before the seed of salvation was planted, we worked the works of the flesh and the one whose seed we carried -- Satan. Now that we are out of the dark and carrying the seed of the one whom chose us, and has sent us -- Jesus we work out our soul salvation with fear and trembling.

As we water the seed of Jesus Christ (the Word), and edify (prophesy) to his spirit within us through our prayer language our fruit is revealed bountifully. Scripture says that out of our bellies shall flow rivers of living water. And faith cometh by hearing and hearing by the word of the Lord. We must read the word and prophesy the word over our unsurrendered soulish life so that we can reach our full measure of faith that is hidden in Christ Jesus.

Francis Frangipane in the "The Three Battlegrounds," writes "If you will truly walk with Jesus, many areas of your thinking process will be exposed...You will see strongholds fall and victory come. But I must warn you, there will be pressure from your flesh, as well as from the demonic world itself, to minimize or ignore what God is requiring of you.

You may be tempted to surrender just a token sin or some minor fault, while allowing you main problems to remain entrenched and well hidden. Let us realize the energies we expend in keeping our sins secret are the actual "materials" of which a stronghold is made. The demon you are fighting is using your thoughts to protect his access to your life."

Think about the areas of your life that God revealed any of the above, and write down the sins that you continue to commit, since you have been saved. Then pray this prayer adapted from Francis Frangipane, calling those sins audibly when you reach them...

"Heavenly Father, there are areas in my life (audibly name the habitual sins) that I have not fully surrendered to my Lord, Jesus Christ. Lord

forgive me of compromise. I also ask you for courage to approach the pulling down of strongholds without reluctance or willful deception in my heart. By the power of the Holy Spirit and in the Name of Jesus, I bind the satanic influences that were reinforcing compromise and sin within me. I submit myself to the light of the Spirit of Truth to expose the strongholds of sin within me. By the mighty weapons of the Spirit and the Word, I proclaim that each stronghold in my life is coming down! I purpose, by the grace of God, to have only one stronghold within me: the stronghold of the Presence of Christ!

I thank You, Lord, for forgiving and cleansing me from all my sins. And by the grace of God, I commit myself to follow through in this area until even the ruins of this stronghold are removed from my mind! Thank You, Father. In Jesus' name. Amen.

Reconciliation

- But now we are no more under the curse of the Law of Sin and Death.

- But now we are able to stand.

- But now we are able to run this race with patience, and finish.

- But now we are released from the power of the Prince of Darkness and the Air.

- But now we are able to live lives wholly separated unto God.

- But now our occupation has been changed to that of Sons, who know their Father's voice and no longer follow the voice of the Stranger.

Have you ever been at a point in your life where you were not where you use to be, but you knew you were not where you were going? That is an in between time, a meanwhile time. When the getting there seems to take a long time. This is a time when the redemptive grace of God is being revealed to us. He speaks in the silence of what seems to a place without a name or an explanation. Redemption is bestowed on us from the throne of grace to first repair the estranged relationship between God and ourselves. Out of that restored relationship comes assurance that we are free in Jesus.

From that point we are no longer at war with ourselves, but at peace -- because we understand that we are not being punished by God.

We are merely undoing the consequences of all the bad choices we have made so far in life. When we have that peace there is a blessed repose, and the bountiful faith that we are changing as we change our environment.

Our Lives after the Cross

Our ability to stand and have a changed nature was accomplished through the fulfillment of many Old Testament Prophecies, and symbolized through the Last Supper.

Isaiah spoke of his coming 750 years plus before his coming. Some Prophets today would be stoned for speaking that prophesy, and it not manifesting by 2 years or less of waiting for his coming.

John 14:30 says 'I'll not be talking with you much more like this because the chief of the godless world is about to attack. But don't worry -- he has nothing on me, no claim on me." (Message Translation, Eugene Peterson)

Remember a vital key is humility. Francis Frangipane, on page 12 in his book "The Three Battlegrounds of the Mind" said, "a vital key to overcoming the devil is humility. To humble yourself is to refuse to defend your image." You are corrupt and full of sin in your old nature! Yet, we have a new nature, which has been created in the likeness of Christ. (Ephesians 4:24). So we can agree with our adversary about the condition of our flesh! The strength of humility is that it builds a spiritual defense around our soul, prohibiting strife, competition and many of life's irritations from stealing our peace.

Galatians 5:21b says, "...of the which I tell you in time past, that they which do such things shall not inherit the kingdom of God."

We are friends and sons. His love flows freely, and he declares in Romans 8:28-39 the following: "And we know that all things work together for the good to them that love God, to them who are the called according to his purpose. For whom he did foreknow, he also did predestinate to be conformed to the image of his Son, that he might be the firstborn among many brethren. Moreover whom he did predestinate, them he also called: and whom he called, them he also justified; and whom he justified them he also glorified. What shall we then say to these things?

If God be for us, who can be against us? He that spared not his own Son, but delivered him up for us all, how shall he not with him also freely give us all things? Who shall lay any thing to the charge of God's elect? It is God that justifieth. Who is he that condemneth? It is Christ that died, yea rather, that is risen again, who is even at the right hand of God, who also maketh intercession for us. Who shall separate us from the love of Christ? Shall tribulation, or distress, or persecution, or famine, or nakedness, or peril, or sword? As it is written, For thy sake we are killed all the daylong: we are accounted as sheep for the slaughter. Nay, in all these things we are more than conquerors through him that loved us. For I am persuaded, that neither death, nor life, nor angels, nor principalities, nor powers, nor things present, nor things to come. Nor height, nor depth, nor any other creature, shall be able to separate us from the love of God, which is in Christ Jesus our Lord."

Chapter 9

A Justified Man

9- A Justified Man -

... Spring Cleaning the Attic

When we spring clean, we first look around the room to ascertain how big of a mess the place is in, then we decide how we are going to clean up the place. We begin to imagine how we want the room to look, and envision it in its finished state. We open the unmarked cluttered boxes in the newly moved into house and rearrange them we can sit and begin to sort through what we have collected.

As we go along we begin to see things from 5, 6, and 7 years ago that have wonderful or painful memories.

A garbage can is pulled out and then we began tossing things away that are no longer needed into a pile and into the garbage can.

Things that are no longer applicable to our current lives, or useful are discarded; hopefully.

We often find photographs of former friends, loves and spouses.

We evaluate if these photos are painful or happy. If they are painful we toss or destroy the memories; and toss out outdated or damaged clothing, or irreparable things. Some throw everything away, to make room to store things in the house, back into the attic. Others will throw away what's in the attic and the house, and start anew. Think about it in terms of the amount of space we allow God to have in our houses, our spiritual bodies for God. Just because it is neatly packed away in a closet, or hung up nicely, and out of mind does not mean that it does not need to be thrown out or repaired.

God wants to fix the broken pieces of our lives (Psalms 31:12) and inhabit every nook and cranny of our living spaces (Psalms 147:3, Jeremiah 18:4). He takes the broken pieces and makes us again, when we surrender to his purpose. The Bible says to those he calls, he justifies (sanctifies) (Romans 8:30). It is the process of sanctification, through his son Jesus Christ and the power of the word of the living God that gives us the root system that causes us to become trees planted by rivers of living water.

Then what is justification to the Christian? According to Romans 8:29-30, it is God's ability to bring out of a person that which is desired, to cause him to appear righteous by fact and not by action. The Pharisees were like this, they believed their works, and attitude of holiness was the offering of sacrificial living that God was requiring; and thus missed their Messiah. (Luke 16:15). Jesus after examining the contents of Paul's house and attic declared him righteous "He had cleansed his heart." Titus 3:5-7, he examines what we hold onto and is aware of every hidden item (sin), and awaits our willingness to cast off and lay aside the thing that holds us captive. "Much more then, being now justified by his blood, we shall be saved from wrath, through him." (Romans 5:9)

"In whom we have redemption through his blood, the forgiveness of sins, according to the riches of his grace. Wherein He hath abounded toward us all wisdom and prudence; Having made known unto the mystery of his will, according to his good pleasure which he hath purposed in himself. That in the dispensation of the fullness of times he might gather together in one all things in Christ, both which are in heaven, and which are on earth; even in him: in whom we have obtained an inheritance, being predestined according to his purpose of him who worketh all things after the counsel of his own will; that we should be to the praise of his glory, who first trusted in Christ." (Ephesians 1:7-12)

When we trust in God, with total reliance upon his ability and provisions made for us through his love, we enter into his rest and find peace. And having made peace through the blood of his cross, by him to reconcile all things unto himself; by him, I say, whether they be things in earth, or things in heaven." (Colossians 1:20) We can increase and have all the places that the soles of our feet tread upon, and have these places become holy through regeneration.

(Obedience)

Examples of Those Who obeyed and possessed their Souls Desires:

Hannah made room for one by fasting and prayer for a son.

Mary made room for one by presenting herself as a living sacrifice.

Boaz made room for one by commanding that provisions be laid aside for his future bride.

Ruth made room for one by accepting God as her God, and received a double portion. God made room for one through his Son Jesus, as a way of escape into sanctification

Widow Zarephath made room for one by sacrificing to the man of God, and received everlasting provisions.

Jesus made room for one by doing away with the veil, emptying himself of his glory and making himself the more excellent way for all to come unto the father.

Mary Magdalene made room by walking away from the lust of the flesh and the pride of life, to find a man who would and did love her beyond what she had experienced and gave her a feeling that was everlasting and not fleeting.

The Woman with the Issue of Blood had been bowed over and loosing her life with every step she took, as the blood coursed out of her body like water being poured from a pitcher. She knew that healing was to be had if she could touch the hem of his garment, what she needed was at his feet and not in his hand that day. The oil flowed from the head to the skirts and gathered there and in her mind, she needed all of him and nothing less to dry up the issues of her life and bring total restoration.

The Woman at the Well had many relations and no legal rights to any man, he told her what only he could tell her and she knew from that moment she had been in the presence of a man like none that she had been with before and that he was 'the man' above all that would satisfy her longings and turn her sorrow into joy. He became her husbandman.

Saul/Paul made room for one by surrendering his authority to God's authority, and received a prize far beyond measurement.

Is and has God revealing and revealed things, stuff and people in your life who have got to go?

Dr. Charles Stanley on one of his programs spoke on obedience. This is not a verbatim account but an abbreviated version, and I believe you will still get the message. It is ours to obey and trust, and God's to respond to the consequences of our obedience and trust. He is obligated to be, His Word to supply our needs. Trust completely, no matter what the word of God is still true. Learn to wait on God's timing and direction as in Isaiah 64:4. Give generously to the Lord's work as in II Corinthians 9. We cannot live the Christian life without Christ living in us. (John 15, Galatians 2:20). God is in absolute control of every circumstance of our lives. (Romans 8:28)

Don't reject God's sovereignty, absolutely depend upon the Holy Spirit for everything. Personal time of meditation should be your time with God. Pray the scriptures, on our knees, not in tangents and fits. Ask Him what he wants us to do. (Joshua 1:6-8, 9).

Enlarging Your Tent Prayer -

Reference Scripture: Isaiah 64:1-12

Having therefore, brethren, boldness to enter into the holiest by the blood of Jesus, by a new and living way, which he hath consecrated for us, through the veil, that is to say, his flesh, and having an high priest over the house of God; let us draw near with a true heart in full assurance of faith, having our hearts sprinkled from an evil conscience, and our bodies washed with pure water. (Hebrews 10:19-22).

The sealer of promise (The Holy Spirit) to everlasting life authorizes us to use the keys of knowledge, binding and loosing. We become inhabitable and prepared to be cohabitants with Christ and our future and present spouses and families.

Binding: Matthew 16:19, and

Loosing: Matthew 18:18

The Lord's Prayer is our model, and it directs us to Adore Him, Seek his divine intervention, Submit to his will, He will give us our needs, Requires us to forgive, and He guides us into deliverance, so that his kingdom and his power and his glory will be performed in us and in the earth as it is in heaven. So that we might walk in righteousness, joy and peace in the Holy Ghost (Matthew 6:13b).

Cleansed and Salted - Ezekiel 16:4

How come only one in ten people, who make a commitment to Christ, are still serving Him 5 years later? Ezekiel gives us some answers:

(1) You must be washed! Your spiritual protection against dirt, disease, and death is "the washing of water by the Word" (Ephesians 5:26). It's not enough to step into the shower every morning " you've also got to step into the Scriptures. Jesus said, Now are ye clean through the word" (Jn 15:3). Sin will keep you from your Bible, and your Bible will keep you from sin. (2) You must be salted! In Hebrew culture, they rubbed salt on newborn babies to toughen their skins so that they could be handled without bruising. Too many of us need "special handling."

We're touchy. If we're corrected, we get defensive. Only when you've been "salted" by mature love and non-legalistic acceptance, can you be really open and honest.

(3) You must be swaddled! When we're first born into God's family, we're vulnerable. We need to be covered and protected.

That's the value of Christian fellowship; it wraps you up tightly in the arms of love and says, "You don't ever have to go back to the old life again! You can begin afresh. You can be healed of your painful past.

You can have good times and good relationships instead of bad ones." Have you been washed, salted, and swaddled?

The Robe of Many Colors

The Relationship (Elohim)

The way the saints are planted is through the storm (whirlwinds). The wind blows seed and pollenates the earth.

The Lord our God has made a coat of many colors for his Son, Jesus to wear. (us) The colors are the nations of saints. Like Joseph's father made him a coat of many colors so he has robed us in his righteousness by wearing us next to himself. The breastplate represented the nations of the 12 Tribes of Israel.

Revelation 19:7 "Let us be glad and rejoice, and give honour to him: for the marriage of the Lamb is come, and his WIFE hath MADE herself ready." And in Matthew 22:1-3

"And Jesus answered and spake unto them by parables, and said, The kingdom of heaven is like unto a certain king, which made a marraiage for his ons, And he sent forth his servants to call them that were bidden to the wedding, and they would not come."

We have been invited to become spouses, sons, friends and witnesses of Him into all the world!

From the foundation of the world he has loved us and planned to redeem us from our bill of divorcement from his presence.

Shall we neglect so great a salvation, or shall we accept the invitation and get dressed for the wedding and find him ready to close the door after we arrive to demonstrate how exclusive the invitation to be in his presence is?

Should you choose to accept then surely you will be willing to commit to the relationship in the marriage to the lamb wholeheartedly and allow him to sustain you from faith to faith and glory to glory!

Glory to Glory – Level of the Relationship

The Outer Court Relationship

Represents the flesh life, the mouth, and/or the body. The physical house that we live in. Psalms 23:6-8, the evil you consume will be vomitted up in your conversation. Isaiah 26:3, the war in the flesh ceases, and the eye is lit up so the body becomes full of light (Luke 11:34-36. Then Jesus acknowledges and abides in our body as His temple, John 2:19, 21, and John 3:6-7. Habakkuk 2:4, the proud heart....the righteous shall live by faith

As part of the structure of the Outer Court, were the steps and the Porch. The Porch was symbolic of the outward (body) and eyes that which is a foreigner in a strange land to the Holy Spirit. God looks inward, man looks outward and is prideful, afraid, deceptive, carnal, lustful, self-controlled, and indecisive.

Yet, he longs to be reunited (but does not know to what). Man misses his first love, and nothing will satisfy but the returning to that first love.

Which means you got to stop hanging out on the porch, and come into the house!

There were 7 steps at the entrance of the Outer Court on Solomons Temple, Ezekiel 40:22-34. Seven is God's number of perfection. The scripture tells us that his grace is sufficient for us, and that his strength is made perfect in our weakness.

At the outset of seeking God, we need his strength to bridge the gap and enable us to seek after him.

The ascent to the Inner Court had 8 steps that led from the Outer Court to the entrance of the Inner Court. The Inner Court is the place of self-denial and the reconciliation of man to God at the Cross of Calvary.

The Brazen Altar and the Laver were the first things the Priest encountered when entering the Inner Court.

The Inner Court Relationship

Represents the souls life that thirst for God. The heart is the window to the soul, and is reflected in the eyes. The mind, reasoning, will and intellect are seated in the heart. God moves on behalf of a perfect heart according to II Chronicles 16:9.

The law converts the soul in Psalms 19:7, rejoices the heart in verse 8, keeps the heart pure in verses 9-10, then the heart is acceptable in verses 11-14. In Psalms 86:11-12, he unites our heart (one). Psalms 23:7, the heart is our true self. A divided heart causes spiritual blindness, Matthew 6:21-23, John 12:39-40. Our sight is restored through Romans 8:4-14, and way made to keep our sight. Ephesians 1:18, eye of mind, the heart is the power of perceiving and understanding.

Brazen Altar

The place for atonement. Which symbolized the need for a blood sacrifice, which Jesus became for the remission of mans sins. The Heart, Mind, and the Soul of man acknowledging his lost state, and the need for redemption. It is at this point man reaches out to God and begins to relinquish control of his will to God.

(Isaiah 64: 1-12)

The place of washing with the water of the word. We acknowledge the hidden sins and desire to be cleansed through and through. It is symbolic of the cleansing power of Jesus, John 13:2-10. The hands and the feet had to be clean on the priest to show they were free from the defilement of sin. The Prince of the Air desires to keep man a slave to sin, but God has made a way of escape through the perfect lamb that was without blemish. Jesus Christ is his name! The tables outlined are meant to draw parallels that will allow you to see what has been accomplished through the death, burial, resurrection and ascension of our Lord Jesus Christ. He has satisfied the thirsty soul and made available to us a water that when drinked no man thirst again.

The Holy Place

The Curtain drawn between the Inner Court and the Holy Place, was meant to separate by gender and nationality. This curtain was torn which did away with the respecter of person. Satan desires to keep you out of fellowship with God.

The articles in the Holy Place, consisted of the Tables of Shewbread, the Candlestick and the Altar of Incense. The Shewbread taught two truths; Christ is our bread, and the Bible is the bread of life for every believer. The Shewbread was the symbol of the provisions for the voids in our emotions to be filled. The Candlestick represented Christ as the light of the world. Only the Spirit can show us the deep things of God.

The Unlimited Presence

Represents the new testament believers full access to abide in the presence of God continually. Luke 10:25-28 Loving God with all of our being. Only He can fulfill the 31,000+ promises because we are one with Him. He will not allow his own to suffer. John 1;1-5, 12-14. At the gate called Beautiful the blind received sight (Jesus, the way, the truth, and the life). In Romans 2:27-29, our hearts are changed as we hear the word and receive it, and are quickened as Christ was quickened.

Hebrews 4:15 all things are laid bare before him. He has given us all power to preach a Gospel that is powerful enough to stand and stop death in our lives. The Body of Christ has received the Jesus on Pilates balcony, the Jesus on the Cross, the Jesus in the Grave. But not the Jesus who went into hell and overthrew Satan, and rolled back the authority of the grave (the stone) and ascended on high and established and restored rightful ownership to the Kingdom of God, over death. I keep saying death, because it is death that has the church in a choke hold. We need to walk in the victory that has been given us to speak to the death in our minds, our homes, our jobs, our finances, our churches and declare that He is Risen from the Dead and He Is Lord!!!! It is a powerless Gospel if we do not preach the authority over the grave! Nothing, and no one can withstand the Lord of Host, who is seated on the right hand of his Father, advocating and interceding and pouring out His spirit into the earth upon the children of God. We are well able to go up and possess the land!

The Veil of the Tabernacle

Separated us from the Holy of Holies from everyone but the High Priest, later torn from top to bottom through Jesus the way into Gods presence.

Ark of the Covenant

Gods' earthly dwelling (spirit) inside were the ten commandments that later become flesh, the Glory of God (Shammah) rested over the Mercy Seat. The testimony, heart and kingdom of God. The hidden treasures, mysteries that are available for revealing his divine presence, blessings, and plans for our lives are shared.

The Ten Commandments

Gods' presence eternally dominating the flesh as original man had dominion over the earth. Oneness, Sanctification, Power, Reconciliation and Inherant Authority.

The Lordship of Jesus has given us a birthright that has come from Abraham down to Jesus, and all the names of those between are laided on top of the others and their giftings, callings and anointings are compressed and packed into us through the Holy Spirit. Job 36:11-12, speaks of the life of obedience. The one who lives this life experience the levels of relationship as they grow from faith to faith and glory to glory. Since, there is no fault in God, the fault lies in us. There is no searching of his ways or his knowledge. Pontius Pilate, could find no fault in Him. How can we blame God for where we are not. When things go differently than we plan or expect – we look for someone to blame. Namely God, he blesses us according to our relationship with him. We have no right to blame my Abba (Daddy) because he has done for me what no man could, has or ever will be able to do, love me in spite of myself unconditionally.

I say like Pontius Pilate, "I find no fault in him." He is perfect in all of his ways, II Samuel 22:3.

For All Times

Isaiah 53: 1 Who hath believed our report? and to whom is the arm of the LORD revealed? 2 For he shall grow up before him as a tender plant, and as a root out of a dry ground: he hath no form nor comeliness; and when we shall see him, there is no beauty that we should desire him. 3 He is despised and rejected of men; a man of sorrows, and acquainted with grief: and we hid as it were our faces from him; he was despised, and we esteemed him not. 4 Surely he hath borne our griefs, and carried our sorrows: yet we did esteem him stricken, smitten of God, and afflicted. 5 But he was wounded for our transgressions, he was bruised for our iniquities: the chastisement of our peace was upon him; and with his stripes we are healed. 6 All we like sheep have gone astray; we have turned every one to his own way; and the LORD hath laid on him the iniquity of us all. 7 He was oppressed, and he was afflicted, yet he opened not his mouth: he is brought as a lamb to the slaughter, and as a sheep before her shearers is dumb, so he openeth not his mouth. 8 He was taken from prison and from judgment: and who shall declare his generation? for he was cut off out of the land of the living: for the transgression of my people was he stricken. 9 And he made his grave with the wicked, and with the rich in his death; because he had done no violence, neither was any deceit in his mouth. 10 Yet it pleased the LORD to bruise him; he hath put him to grief: when thou shalt make his soul an offering for sin, he shall see his seed, he shall prolong his days, and the pleasure of the LORD shall prosper in his hand. 11 He shall see of the travail of his soul, and shall be satisfied: by his knowledge shall my righteous servant justify many; for he shall bear their iniquities. 12 Therefore will I divide him a portion with the great, and he shall divide the spoil with the strong; because he hath poured out his soul unto death: and he was numbered with the transgressors; and he bare the sin of many, and made intercession for the transgressors.

In the years before our birth, there were many who would be considered ignoble persons who have made it into the lineage of Jesus. Each whose name has a symbolic meaning reflecting the nature of Gods' mercy and love for us. When the Bible says in Isaiah 53 of the iniquities, griefs, sorrows, transgressions, chastisements, peace and judgment was all being reconciled through him from generations before to allow us free access into God's presence. There is a visual of him passing through the annals of time in my mind and picking out the wheat and tare of every ancestral line to be conceived and weaving them into the fabric of his passion. He knew that there would be no other way to wholely perform his Fathers will but to suffer for all of man. Look at some of the names that are included in the lineage of Jesus Christ and their names meanings and see the plan of God to make sure that you and I were not left out of the redemption plan that I have found all point to the sinner we were and the sons we have now become through Jesus Christ.

Chapter 10

Where there is

Bitterness

10- Where There is Bitterness

By nature bitterness is a belief-system that clouds our judgment of people and situations.

A story quoted that "Bitterness is not just a wound seeking healing, it is a prosecuting attorney building a case against the guilty. Because a bitter soul is conjoined to the injustice committed against it, it perpetually is listening to the voice of its heartache and, thus, perpetually wounded by the unforgiven offense."

Deal with this bitterness, let the Lord touch it, otherwise you will not be able to receive HIS authority to overcome. Perhaps you have hidden bitterness towards men or women, or certain races. If you lost a loved one, perhaps your grief turned bitter.

When the deep root of bitterness gets exposed, there are intense disappointments that must be grieved. Many of us avoid this sadness because grief is difficult to enter. Many of us who know that we are wounded in a certain area and admit it but cannot grieve, because when you touch that sadness it feels uncontrollable.

Not only is there grieving, there is also repentance. Another story quoted about "…why the priests were not allowed to minister in the temple if they had scabs. The scabs were a prophetic symbol of the places of injury that are not completely healed, and therefore are capable of muddling our hearing from God, our ministering to others, our heart. Many people mistake the voice of their inner bitterness for the voice of God (and often this is where the demonic can masquerade as the voice of God, too). I used to experience this quite often, when I was first really understanding how God speaks to me.

The priests were "unclean" if they had scabs.

They had to enter a prolonged period of healing before they could return to the temple. We too need to create space for grief and healing. A scab is a healing wound, but it is still able to be penetrated again, and therefore can spread infection.

Bitterness is a perpetual scab that is consistently reinfected.

The way to know, I think, that you have been delivered from bitterness (when the scab is gone) is when you experience a familiar disappointment or injustice and you no longer feel victimized or retreat or blame others. You think the best of your friends and enemies, even if there is pain that needs to be discussed....The waters of Marah (bitterness) become sweet. What once was bitter is a place for joy. Only when we yield this bitterness to him will we be able to be persecuted and know the meaning of this: "Blessed are you when people insult you and persecute you, and falsely say all kinds of evil against you because of Me. Moving from bitterness to joy will allow us to rejoice and be glad and leap for joy, for your reward in heaven is great" (Matt. 5:11-12).

It is a spiritual law not a principle that if we draw close to God, He will draw close to us. This means that it is a way that Reality is set up, that when people draw close to God, ...by His Nature draws near to us.

There are ways of ascending into heaven. These are practical and taught in scripture. The most obvious maps are in David's writings. We need to know practical ways of entering God's Realm. Many people are entering heaven more often than before through worship and in dream and visions in our day, but few have been shown the basic maps of how to ascend and enter.

Here are practical tools for ascending. They are found in scripture and follow this pattern. First, we confess all our sins, for, "who may ascend the hill of the Lord? He who has clean hands and a pure heart." (Ps.24:3) Jesus did this for us at the cross.

So we start there--with the cross. Because when we confess our sins He is faithful to forgive and cleanse, this is the way we begin our ascent--through confession. This is because sin blocks us from being able to be fully in God's Presence. So we confess.

When we do this, we realize what He has done and then enter thanks. We find ourself thanking Him for cleansing us--for the cross--and for the present application of the cross. Once we are thanking Him, we enter the courts--ie the outer parts of heaven. For thankfulness creates a space in us which allows God to flow and move us.

Once we are thanking, we enter, and once we enter His Courts, we will then find ourselves praising Him. That is the order of ascension: confession, thanks, praise. You see this pattern also in Daniel's prayer life, and in the Lord's prayer.

Once we are praising, God can take us anywhere in heaven and show us whatever He wishes us to see. He may show us our heavenly homes, or the parts of heaven that we are meant to, and will eventually completely, dwell within. Or, He may show us His Feet. He may show us something He is doing in a friend's life, or for a group or nation of people. But He will show us things! This may be a space where He shows us how He is praying for someone or a place, and so may bring intercession. Or it may be a place of gazing on some aspect of Himself. Whatever he leads us to we will go there and enter!

This is a simple pattern of entry, but it is practical. In our hour, many are being drawn up into heaven on a more regular basis, and this is for His Purposes. But we need to know these basic patterns or laws of The Spirit, so we will not become confused.

Many for instance, go worship once a week, and as they leave find themselves passing back into a spiritual valley of shadow.

This is to be expected. For as we pass back through the gates of heaven, the enemy's hordes are outside of these gates, and they attempt to get us to focus on them, and leave the streams or ways of God pouring out from heaven.

Know that on the outside of the gates, the enemy gathers--both to keep people out, and to keep people from returning, and to try to steal the things which one has gathered from heaven.

Once we know that this is the case, we are less immediately drawn away from the streams or ways or righteousness (the still waters) that keep us in the ways of God. The enemy is always trying to draw us out away from those streams.

But to stay by them is a matter of staying close to the good shepherd as we descend into the valleys.

We are to do whatever we is lawful for us to do to stay close to Jesus. He has made a way of escape for us and reconciled the generations. Through the lineage of Jesus you see that there are character flaws amongst those in his genealogy.

We see both men and women who were guilty of various sins, and it is through the represented presence in his lineage that we see the true ministry of reconciliation. God was in Jesus reaching down through time reconciling the world unto himself. Look at the list below and see…

What Is In the Name of Jesus' Lineage

- Elohim - God of Relationships
- Abram(ham) – exalted father of a multitude
- Ishmael – war
- Isaac – laughter and God will hear
- Jacob – heel catcher, supplanter, God protects
- Judah – may he "God" be praised
- Perez – breach
- Zerah – dawning, rising and shining
- Hezron - shut in, blooming or dart of joy
- Aram – exalted
- Amminadab – people of liberality
- Nahshon - enchanting or ominous
- Salmon - peaceable
- Boaz – fleetness (to be nimble)
- Rahab – (broad, wide) Grk. Insolence, pride
- and violence in the Hebrew
- Obed – serving
- Ruth – a female friend
- Jesse - Jehovah exists or firm
- David – beloved or chieftain
- Solomon – peaceable in the Hebrew, also called Jedidiah beloved of Jehovah
- Bathsheba – daughter of the oath
- Rehoboam – enlarger of the people
- Abijah – God is my father or "daddy"
- Asa – healing, to heal, a physician
- Jehosophat –Jehovah judged
- Joram – Jehovah is high
- Uzziah – Jehovah is strength

- Jotham – Jehovah is upright
- Ahaz – possessor
- Hezekiah – Jehovah is strength
- Manasseh – causing to forget
- Amon – faithful
- Josiah – Jehovah heads
- Jehoiachin – Jehovah will establish
- Shealtiel – I have asked God
- Zerubbabel – Seed (progeny)
- Abiud – Father of renown
- Eliakim – God will establish
- Azar – helper
- Ehud - strong or union
- Eleazar – God is helper
- Matthan - a gift
- Jacob - supplanter or followeth after
- Joseph – may he Jehovah add
- Mary – obstinancy, rebellion

2 Corinthians 5:17-21 (KJV)

"Therefore if any man *be* in Christ, *he is* a new creature: old things are passed away; behold, all things are become new. 18 And all things *are* of God, who hath reconciled us to himself by Jesus Christ, and hath given to us the ministry of reconciliation; 19 To wit, that God was in Christ, reconciling the world unto himself, not imputing their trespasses unto them; and hath committed unto us the word of reconciliation. 20 Now then we are ambassadors for Christ, as though God did beseech *you* by us: we pray *you* in Christ's stead, be ye reconciled to God. 21 For he hath made him *to be* sin for us, who knew no sin; that we might be made the righteousness of God in him."

He covered all of our personalities and hang-ups and races. Culminating to the point in time where God would no longer go before us as a pillar or over us as a cloud, but in us through the Holy Spirit to comfort us and come along side of us to lead and guide us into all truth. Not even being a member of the Old Testament patriarchy was sufficient to exempt us from the need for redemption. We were forced to rely on the man who would make it through to the Holy of Holies without dying on the way to make atonement for us once a year. This High Priest Jesus Christ did not die on the way to offer the sacrifice for us! He made it to and through the offering up of himself on our behalf for our predecessors and ourselves who dwelt in the outer court. We are to be one as the Father and Jesus are one through the sanctity of the way that has been made for us through the

Inner Court Relationship

John 17:17-26 Jesus is praying to the Father,

"**Sanctify** them through thy truth: thy word is truth. 18 As thou hast sent me into the world, even so have I also sent them into the world. 19 And for their sakes I sanctify myself, that they also might be sanctified through the truth to **glorify them,** and all other believers with Him in heaven 20 Neither pray I for these alone, but for them also which shall believe on me through their word; 21 That they **all may be one**; as thou, Father, art in me, and I in thee, that they

<u>also may be one in</u> us: that the world may believe that thou hast sent me. 22 <u>And the glory which thou gavest me I have given them; that they may be one, even as we are one:</u> 23 I in them, and thou in me, that they may be made perfect in one; and that the world may know that thou hast sent me, and hast loved them, as thou hast loved me. 24 Father, I will that they also, whom thou hast given me, be with me where I am; that they may behold my glory, which thou hast given me: for thou lovedst me before the foundation of the world. 25 Father, the world hath not known thee: but I have known thee, and these have known that thou hast sent me. 26 And I have declared unto them thy name, and will declare it: that the love wherewith thou hast loved me may be in them, and I in them."

Now we all can go from one level to the next as we are inclined to follow and remain in his presence forever. I John 2:1-4, if you love me keep (do) my commandments. He commanded blessings on us and then showed us the way to the blessing. He gave the commandments to the earth to respond when we obey. The earth is the Lord's according to Deuteronomy 28, 29, you will be blessed in the city and in the field, …if we will be willing and obedient we would eat the good of the land.

This state of wellness for you and your household that Jesus fulfilled from the Old Testament and brought it forward into the New Testament: (Leviticus 25:10, 18. Galatians 3:22, Romans 11:36, and Colossians 1:19-20. II Timothy 2:11-13) These words are nchanging, it is a trustworthy statement, that if we are faithless he remains faithful, for he cannot deny himself. Psalms 25:14 the secret of the Lord. He wants us to know Him – be intimately acquainted with his tender loving mercy.

Revelations 1:5-6 and Lamentations 3:37,39 and Matthew 11:6, says our relationship takes us out of the state of living for and by miracles; and moves us into the realm of blessings. The realm of blessings is a place of continual care, and not the state of dependency on the suddenly of miracles. Miracles are needed assistance from God. Blessings are a commanded state of wellness for you and your household.

John 3:14-15 tells us clearly, "As Moses lifted up the serpent in the wilderness, even so must the Son of man be lifted up: that whosoever believeth in him should not perish, but have eternal life." To look with the external eyes and believe with the internal eyes of the heart. Faith to believe unto salvation comes by seeing with the eyes of the soul (external) and comprehending the saving God with the (internal) eyes. Keeping our inward eyes on the Father as Jesus did in Matthew 14:19 "Looking up to heaven, he blessed, and brake, and gave bread to his disciples" when he raised Lazarus from the tomb in John 11:41,"Then they took away the stone from the place where the dead was laid. And Jesus lifted up his eyes, and said, Father, I thank thee that thou hast heard me."

Throughout the ministry of Jesus you find him looking up and this is the way we learn to abide in Him. We look up to block out the external distractions from us. Now you cannot walk always looking up literally, but figuratively your Spirit man that has been empowered desires to do the looking up for you. Keep the Holy Spirit empowered comes from feeding on the Word of God, Prayer, Praise and Worship of God until you are satisfied that when you pray God hears you! There is a time when the quantity time you spend with God becomes the quality time you receive back from God. Quantity precedes quality. Nothing in the bank – nothing out of the bank!

Making deposits into your relationship with God before you need Him!

Through believing on the Lord Jesus Christ and looking unto Jesus the author and finisher of our faith as in Hebrews 12:2 direct the heart to focus on Jesus continuously. Taking your mind from its natural tendency to focus on itself and onto the Lamb of God! We intentionally focus our attention on Jesus, not always being able to maintain that focus due to external distractions for which God already knows about. God takes allowance for that as we grow in grace and does not condemn us for our wavering thoughts as new believers. There does come a time as you are mature in Christ Jesus that you will have formed a habit of focusing on God through Jesus Christ until it has become second nature. The things of the world cannot prevent you from getting into His presence when you sense his desire is to have more of you. This is where you decrease and he increases in your relationship. Your focus moves away from your will and more onto what is required of you from Him. To climb into heaven we must take our focus off of ourselves and how wretched we are and before long the sin conscious soul becomes righteousness conscious and the mind that was in Christ Jesus has now become the mind which rest in you! While you are looking at God through Jesus Christ and gazing at them they are touching you in the secret places of your soul! He reaches inward to us and we must reach outward to Him. We live in this world but we are not of this world, the world requires we focus on the issues of the day, but the heart of your spirit longs to be in Gods' presence. At first opportunity you find yourself rushing back to get into Him. Sounds like a relationship with someone you really want to be with! When you want to be with Him as much as He wants to be with you, seconds away seem like hours!

He knows you have to attend to the affairs of this life, but there is a secret place inside of you that senses that you are tied to Him even while you are sitting at your desk, cooking that meal. This is the joy of the Lord because you know without provocation that yours is a special relationship just between the two of you. He is devoted to you and you are devoted to Him! What shall separate you from this love – nothing!

The Fear of the Lord

There is no distance in your relationship and no walls of separation in the divine order of the relationship you have with God! They only exist in your own heart and mind. When Adam and Eve were afraid and fearful of God after the fall it was due to their own consciousness. They were naked before the fall and unashamed before God. After the fall their nakedness become a shameful thing to them, not to God! This is not the fear of the Lord we speak of in this instance. That fear was due to guilt and shame from disobedience. The fear of the Lord is to find yourself on common ground with God about how He sees things. God saw Adam and Eves failure to keep the only commandment He had given them and the penalty for their disobedience would cause a break in their relationship. They were self-aware creatures now and were uncomfortable before their creator. This is the inheritance of the wicked -- that is the fear of godliness. When Adam and Eve fell they hid (became deceptive) which was the result of coming into contact with the deceiver.

The result was a trail of broken relationships; with God themselves, broken relationships; with God, themselves, the earth and the things in the earth.

Reverence of God

Disobedience will cause us to lose reverence for God and the things of God. When we reverence God; how does it differ from having the fear of God? When we are deceptive we hide from God and that is what Adam and Eve did. This broken commandment carried a five fold sentence (the curse) of serpent, satan, woman, man and the earth.

Then God blessed the Earth in Genesis 2:74,

Genesis 1:28, Genesis 2:5, but Cursed Man

Genesis 3:16-19 and Genesis 3:14-15.

When God makes a request of us and we fail to honor that request for whatever reason; we are irreverent. Render unto God what is required of God! More than anything else he asks us to follow these guidelines found in Deuteronomy 30:16-20, "In that I command thee this day to love the LORD thy God, to walk in his ways, and to keep his commandments and his statutes and his judgments, that thou mayest live and multiply: and the LORD thy God shall bless thee in the land whither thou goest to possess it. 17 But if thine heart turn away, so that thou wilt not hear, but shalt be drawn away, and worship other gods, and serve them; 18 I denounce unto you this day, that ye shall surely perish, and that ye shall not prolong your days upon the land, whither thou passest over Jordan to go to possess it. 19 I call heaven and earth to record this day against you, that I have set before you life and death, blessing and cursing: therefore choose life, that both thou and thy seed may live: 20 That thou mayest love the LORD thy God, and that thou mayest obey his voice, and that thou mayest cleave unto him: for he is thy life, and the length of thy days: that thou mayest dwell in the land which the LORD sware unto thy fathers, to Abraham, to Isaac, and to Jacob, to give them."

Authority and Fatherhood

Gathering ourselves together in corporate prayer, corporate worship and corporate service are all things God desires of us. Yet, it is the private prayer, private worship and private service to God that aligns us and prepares us for corporate fellowship. God wants you to be so into Him; that should the doors of the church in your community close or your means of transportation fail, or something requiring you to move to a distant place without a local body of believers you will not falter in your faith. You have learned of Him and are able to commune with him wherever you are. Because you know that your relationship is not tied to a physical building but to the True and Living God! Should you find yourself in this place today, here is a prayer for you – "O Lord, I have been tempted to look away from you today, but I chose to look away to you and respond to your call with my whole heart.

Cleanse me of all unrighteousness and create in me a clean heart and renew a right spirit within me. Pull the scales off of my eyes that have clouded my eyes that has weakened my ability to see myself as you see me and to see you as you truly are. Wash me and purge me with your blood and keep me with my eyes of my heart fixed upwardly on you, In Jesus Name – Amen.

Sonship and Obedience

Numbers 6:22-27

22 And the LORD spake unto Moses, saying, 23 Speak unto Aaron and unto his sons, saying, On this wise ye shall bless the children of Israel, saying unto them, 24 The LORD bless thee, and keep thee: 25 The LORD make his face shine upon thee, and be gracious unto thee: 26 The LORD lift up his countenance upon thee, and give thee peace. 27 And they shall put my name upon the children of Israel; and I will bless them.

There is an understanding of the Lord as the one Who IS and IS forever and keeps us because he neither slumbers nor sleeps and that his intent over our lives is that we would be one. John declares the unique love of God toward us, in making us His children. I John 3:1-3 says, Behold, what manner of love the Father hath bestowed upon us, that we should be called the sons of God: therefore the world knoweth us not, because it knew him not. 2 Beloved, now are we the sons of God, and it doth not yet appear what we shall be: but we know that, when he shall appear, we shall be like him; for we shall see him as he is. 3 And every man that hath this hope in him purifieth himself, even as he is pure.

I John 3:10 says, In this the children of God are manifest, and the children of the devil: whosoever doeth not righteousness is not of God, neither he that loveth not his brother. 11 For this is the message that ye heard from the beginning, that we should love one another. 12 Not as Cain, who was of that wicked one, and slew his brother. And wherefore slew he him? Because his own works were evil, and his brother's righteous. 13 Marvel not, my brethren, if the world hate you. 14 We know that we have passed from death unto life, because we love the brethren. He that loveth not his brother abideth in death. 15 Whosoever hateth his brother is a murderer: and ye know that no murderer hath eternal life abiding in him. 16 Hereby perceive we the love of God, because he laid down his life for us: and we ought to lay down our lives for the brethren. 17 But whoso hath this world's good, and seeth his brother have need, and shutteth up his bowels of compassion from him, how dwelleth the love of God in him? 18 My little children, let us not love in word, neither in tongue; but in deed and in truth. 19 And hereby we know that we are of the truth, and shall assure our hearts before him. 20 For if our heart condemn us, God is greater than our heart, and knoweth all things. 21 Beloved, if our heart condemn us not, then have we confidence toward God. 22 And whatsoever we ask, we receive of him, because we keep his commandments, and do those things that are pleasing in his sight. 23 And this is his commandment, That we should believe on the name of his Son Jesus Christ, and love one another, as he gave us commandment. 24 And he that keepeth his commandments dwelleth in him, and he in him. And hereby we know that he abideth in us, by the Spirit which he hath given us.

In this age of foreclosures and bankruptcy, accept this word from God – that he has taken your soul out of foreclosure and bankruptcy through Jesus Christ! Disappointments come but all you have to do is stay on the right side of the comma and watch God work it out for you!

God is going to establish the Word of God in your life that you choose to embrace and give you revelation and establish your steps. He wants you to walk in victory through your covenant relationship. This is shaking the dust off or yourself so that God will stand you up at the gate of your soul as High Priest through Jesus Christ, and change you forever toward the kingdom of God. A place of posterity for your generations is what he has had on his mind all alone; according to Jeremiah 29:11.

But we serve a God who will not let us be tempted above that which we can bear! Because He knows the way we take and the frame he has made for us to bear up. His yoke is easy and his burden is light! We have been deceived by Satan and taken on a false-burden onto our frame and a yoke of silver about our necks that weigh us down and beset us. Let us lay aside every weight and sin that doth so easily beset us!

He desires for us to prosper above all things, be in health, even as our soul prospers. Gods' way of bringing us into success is a balanced way of living as he has ordained for us to live! He is not an extremist or out of balance!

As his children when we take our journey we are to mark the first Son of God and walk becoming as Sons of God. From determining that you will serve Him and seek Him "With Oneness of Heart" and "Journey this Road of Oneness Intentionally" so that when you meet up with the "Detours of life that would call you off the Road of Oneness" you are a wise and cunning servant who knows the devices of the enemy that would keep you from an enviable relationship of being able to say that "I and My Father Are One" in purpose! I do what brings honor to God with the ultimate goal in sight of pleasing Him! Who would dare not to be in the presence of such a relationship? When you see this kind of relationship success in the natural it is to be admired, but to be this relationship! Well that is when the aroma of your praise and your worship come before God as a sweet smelling savor! He no longer smells the stinch of sin of the old man, but the fragrance of a heart that wants more of God with each passing day! What a privilege and an honor to know that he enjoys smelling our relationship! The smell of you excites God! WOW! Imagine finally, being totally free from your past, things done to you and by you we can be naked and unashamed with God!

The Fragrance of the Relationship

The Root of Bitterness prevents growth. Bitterness carries the seeds of resentment, hatred, unforgiveness, violence, temper, retaliation, murder, jealousy, selfishness, rebellion, and accusation. The fragrance of these things are released as the winds of change blow in our lives. As the rose gives off its' fragrance when fanned so does the tree whose roots are bitterness.

The fragrance of the Root of Jesus promotes growth. The Word says that except a seed fall into the grown and die it abides alone. Jesus was the root of Jesse, and the seed that fell into the earth, the tomb and died a natural death so that the seed of faith could be released when he arose. This relationship is released as our graft is intermingled with the vine. The way the saints of God are planted is through the storms (whirlwinds) that carry the seeds and pollinates the earth. The Lord our God has made a coat of many colors for his son, Jesus to wear. The colors are the nations of people. Like Josephs' father made him a coat of many colors, so he has with us robed us in his righteousness by wearing us next to himself. The breastplate represented the nations of the twelve tribes of Israel.

The ark is a statement of relationship as God instructed Noah, and he obeyed. When Noah had done all to stand, he stood inside of the ark of safety. Sealed within and sealed without by the pitch between the boards. That pitch was prophetically symbolizing the blood of Jesus that would enclose us in his covenant love. He abides in us as the pitch abides within the planks, and without as we abide within him.

Traditions of man say that the order is God, Country, Family and Job. The Godly order of relationships is God first, and all things are fitted in him. We order our lives in God not around God. All things exist in Him. The Salvation of God (Soteria),

Sozo, safe, delivered, made whole, preserved from danger, loss and destruction, to keep alive. It occurs 54 times in the gospel as to rescue from death of which occurs 14 times. It relates to deliverance from disease or demon possession.

20 times rescue of physical life from peril or instant death. 20 referencing spiritual salvation.

In Psalms 30, we find the answer to Micah 7:8, and Psalms 32. The Song of Solomon is a love affair, which equals our salvation. The lover of our souls. I am today all together lovely, radiant, loved, I am his and he is mine.

Flies in the Ointments Ecclesiastes 10:1

Some types of flies in the ointment of Solomon are doubt, pride and selfishness all which lead us to paths of self-destruction. God is jealous and no other god will he tolerate as interference in your relationship including the relationship with yourself. He desires us to live in the "Zoe" the God life which is found in the kingdom of God relationship of Righteousness, Joy and Peace in the Holy Ghost. A divided heart is the throne room of Satan. It is full of unrighteousness, death, turmoil and the Anti-Christ life that is against God. Self-victimization prevents us from having rest and peace in God. Being in Him is due to our relating with him and not to Him. We can not identify with him as a man does to a man, but must find our identity in Him as we are occupants in him. While we are in Him, he is getting inside of us.

After being inside of the unity of the trinity where Father, Son and Holy Spirit are on one accord we come forth persuaded to stand in the God-life.

Pre-Extrication

Extricate means to unravel, to distinguish from a related thing, to free or remove from an entanglement or difficulty. The synonyms for extricate are disentangle, untangle, disencumber, disembarass and to free from what binds or holds back.

A Time of Death and Bondage

Under the curse of the law we were constantly falling, and failing to finish the course before us. We were caught up in the world and its devices, children of Satan who were constantly in a state of disobedience and under his control. The old man fulfilled the works of the flesh because his spirit was governed by the Prince of Darkness. We lived a life devoted to being led by our own passions and lusts. We were sinners by occupation to the sins of lust, divination, false worship and anger.

Sins of Lust

Adultery being unlawful sex between married person other than their mate. Fornication being unlawful sex between persons who are unmarried. Uncleanness being homosexuality, pornography, masturbation, erotica, bestiality, rape, incest, exploitation and raping of children.

Lasciviousness being out of control desires and lewd behavior and acting out lewd fantasies.

Sins of Divination and False Worship

Idolatry being worship of statues, picture and images. Witchcraft conjuring up evil spirits to communicate with and through spells, charms, amulets worn on the body or clothing to ward off or welcome the presence of evil spirits. Inflicting evil upon others through enchantments or to control ones behavior for or against persons.

Sins of Anger

Hatred to the point of bitter dislike, abhorrence, ill thought and hopes on others and holding grudges. Variance creating dissensions, discord, quarreling, debating and disputes. Emulations of jealousy and competition. Wrath that is rage and anger that lingers to the point of creating turmoil and vengeance.

Strife filled words with the intent to payback in kind wrongs done to them. Seditions that form cliques, stirring up junk and mess everywhere. Heresies where the truth is not accepted but has its own interpretation. Envyings that promote ill will and jealousy at the good fortune of others. Murders where we seek the destruction of another's life and happiness.

Sins of the Stomach

Drunkenness that places you in bondage to alcohol and drugs. Reveling that form riots, obscenities and uninhibited feasting and partying.

All of these are things that the prodigal son experienced in his separation from his fathers house and blessings. Yet, the brother who remained home failed to exercise the benefits provided to him.

The Prodigal Son and the Older Brother

The older brother is symbolic of the believer trying to earn the free gift of a life in Jesus Christ. It is free – the gift is yours to take and open and use as often as you desire! We take the Soul with its inferiority, insecurity, inadequacies, guilt, shame and how we think and feel about ourselves and submit it to the Spirit of God through accepting Salvation that brings with it an assurance of being securely placed in the Kingdom as one who is accepted in the Beloved. He is yours and you are His – a relationship of total commitment. You are a spirit and what is to be desired is that spirit-to-spirt relationship with The Spirit of the Living God! No other relationship has so much to offer you as this relationship does! Intimacy with God comes through Sanctification; which is fellowship and union of spirit until the point that the lesser abdicates the throne in full intention of following the rules of engagement in the relationship with the only wise God our Savior!

Post-extrication

Our ability to stand and have a changed natture was accomplished through the fulfillment of many Old Testament prophecies and symbolized through the Last Supper. Isaiah spoke of his coming 750 years plus before he actually arrived. Some Prophets today would be stoned for speaking that prophesy and it not manifesting by 2 years or less after it had been spoken.

Galatians 5:21b says, "...of the which I tell you in time past, tht they which do such things shall not inherit the kingdom of God."

But now we are no more under the curse of the law of sin and death, but able to stand, and run this race with patience to the finish.

We are now released from the power of Satan

and able to live lives wholly separated unto God. In Ephesians the believer is growing and waxing stronger everyday, no longer making excuses and blaming other people for their behavior and lack. They do not turn back, but allow the fire power of the Word of God to remove the dross (death) out of their spirits and become full of the presence of the life God as originally intended. Our eyes, ears and heart have an understanding that they are no longer the passageway for Satan and his maggot filled trash in their lives. The flies are out of the ointment and the fragrance from the apothecary is "Excellence"!

Ephesians Chapter 1:3-14says,

"Blessed be the God and Father of our Lord Jesus Christ, who hath blessed us with all spiritual blessings in heavenly places in Christ: 4 According as he hath chosen us in him before the foundation of the world, that we should be holy and without blame before him in love: 5 Having predestinated us unto the adoption of children by Jesus Christ to himself, according to the good pleasure of his will, 6 To the praise of the glory of his grace, wherein he hath made us accepted in the beloved. 7 In whom we have redemption through his blood, the forgiveness of sins, according to the riches of his grace; 8 Wherein he hath abounded toward us in all wisdom and prudence; 9 Having made known unto us the mystery of his will, according to his good pleasure which he hath purposed in himself: 10 That in the dispensation of the fulness of times he might gather together in one all things in Christ, both which are in heaven, and which are on earth; even in him: 11 In whom also we have obtained an inheritance, being predestinated according to the purpose of him who worketh all things after the counsel of his own will: 12 That we should be to the praise of his glory, who first trusted in Christ. 13 In whom ye also trusted, after that ye heard the word of truth, the gospel of your salvation: in whom also after that ye believed, ye were sealed with that holy Spirit of promise, 14 Which is the earnest of our inheritance until the redemption of the purchased possession, unto the praise of his glory. "

No longer would we need someone to point the way to God, but we would hear his voice and follow. He is no longer silent or has his back turned to us. We no longer live outside the presence of God like dogs, foreigners and scape goats, but we come boldly before his presence as Queen Esther did and ask what we will of Him. We have had the stone of reproach rolled away from us and taken out of the tomb. We have now tasted the honey in the rock and drank of the water springing forth from the rock of our redemption. He has pulled us up out of the cracked cisterns of Jeremiah where water seeped in and caused the dirt to become sinking sand.

We could not get our balance and until he became the manifested rock of our salvation. He told Peter that he would build his church "You and I" upon that rock so that the gates of hell would not prevail against us! The keys to the kingdom have been issued and our live are hidden in Christ. We are constant and instant in season and out of season. We run the race with patience and we know whose we are!

In the Care of God

Zechariah 2:1-13 God, in His care for Jerusalem, sends a man to measure it. 1 I lifted up mine eyes again, and looked, and behold a man with a measuring line in his hand. 2 Then said I, Whither goest thou? And he said unto me, To measure Jerusalem, to see what is the breadth thereof, and what is the length thereof. 3 And, behold, the angel that talked with me went forth, and another angel went out to meet him, 4 And said unto him, Run, speak to this young man, saying, Jerusalem shall be inhabited as towns without walls for the multitude of men and cattle therein: 5 For I, saith the LORD, will be unto her a wall of fire round about, and will be the glory in the midst of her. 6 Ho, ho, come forth, and flee from the land of the north, saith the LORD: for I have spread you abroad as the four winds of the heaven, saith the LORD. 7 Deliver thyself, O Zion, that dwellest with the daughter of Babylon. 8 For thus saith the LORD of hosts; After the glory hath he sent me unto the nations which spoiled you: for he that toucheth you toucheth the apple of his eye. 9 For, behold, I will shake mine hand upon them, and they shall be a spoil to their servants: and ye shall know that the LORD of hosts hath sent me. 10 Sing and rejoice, O daughter of Zion: for, lo, I come, and I will dwell in the midst of thee, saith the LORD. 11 And many nations shall be joined to the LORD in that day, and shall be my people: and I will dwell in the midst of thee, and thou shalt know that the LORD of hosts hath sent me unto thee. 12 And the LORD shall inherit Judah his portion in the holy land, and shall choose Jerusalem again. 13 Be silent, O all flesh, before the LORD: for he is raised up out of his holy habitation.

The Zoe

When we are standing in the Trinity we are enclosed and encircled from within and without. Surrounded by their unity the old man in us is squeezed out like the pressing of the olive. The unity of God is entering us and removing the division. As our flesh yields to this process we are changed into His image and likeness from the inside out. We have been redeemed and delivered by Jesus Christ the Messiah! He delivered us from the bondage of sin and death forever. He made us unleavened through His broken body and shed blood as witnessed to in I

Corinthians 5:7-8. God kept His promise to us made in Exodus 6:6-7, "Say therefore to the sons of Israel, I am the LORD, and I will bring you out from under the burdens of the Egyptians (sanctification) and I will deliver you from their bondage (judgment) and I will also redeem you with an outstretched arm and with great judgments (redemption) then I will take you for My people and I will be your God (praise). We have been extricated from bondage and into the position of Sons. Kenneth E. Hagin said, "Get thrilled with the Word of God. Walk in the light of it. Claim what the Word promises and you will reap its benefits. When you become a doer of the Word, not a hearer only, you will become a recipient of all the provisions God made for you in His Word."

Endnotes

MATERIALS
Bibles: King James Version

Books:

Myles Munroe, copyright 1991
Single, Married, Separated & Life After Divorce
Bahamas Faith Ministries Published by Vincom, Inc.
P.O. Box 702400
Tulsa, OK 74170
Reprint Permission Granted by Vincom, Inc.

Eugenia Price

Woman to Woman, copyright 1959

Zondervan Books
Zondervan Publishing House
Grand Rapids, MI 49506
Used by Permission of Zondervan Publishing House

Derek and Ruth Prince

God Is A Matchmaker, 1986
Chosen Books a Division of Baker Book House
P.O. Box 6287
Grand Rapids, MI 49516-6287
Used by Permission of Baker Book House

Spiros Zodhiates

The Complete Word Study – New Testament
Chattanooga, TN 37422
AMG Publishers, 1991
6815 Shallowford Rd.
Box 22000
Reprint Permission Granted by AMG Publishers

Volumes in the One Heart Series

VOLUME 1
With Oneness of Heart: Preparing to Regain My Original Position in Life
ISBN 0-9700976-0-3
Formats: Paper, Audio, E-Book & Digital, Kindle

VOLUME 2
Journeying to the Road Called Oneness: To Regain My Original Position in Life
ISBN 0-9700976-1-1
Formats: Paper, Audio, E-Book & Digital, Kindle

VOLUME 3
Detouring off the Road of Oneness: Away from My Original Position in Life
ISBN 0-9700976-2-X
Formats: Paper, Audio, E-Book & Digital, Kindle

VOLUME 4
I and My Father Are One: Abiding in My Regained Position
ISBN 0-9700976-3-8
Formats: Paper, Audio, E-Book & Digital, Kindle

VOLUME 5
One Heart Series Devotional 52 Weeks: Sustaining My Regained Position in Life
ISBN 09700976-7-0
Formats: Paperback

Other Books by Patricia E. Adams

Set Free to Praise Him: A Childs' Rights Violated Her Terrors and Traumas
ISBN 0-9700976-5-4

Salvation "Soteria" Unpack It and Use It, It's More Than a Ticket To Heaven
ISBN 0-9700976-4-6

Shortcuts Consequences Integrity on the Line: Will You Take the Low Road or the High Road
ISBN 0-9700976-6-2

Help My Fears Shadow is Chasing Me (PTSD) Traumas Aftershock
ISBN 0-9700976-8-9

Fiery Darts of the Assassin: Know the Nature of the Enemy Satan
ISBN 0-9700976-9-7

www.ingramcontent.com/pod-product-compliance
Lightning Source LLC
Chambersburg PA
CBHW071017240426
43661CB00073B/2338